A love story of

Mario and Barbara

I would especially like to thank our friend, Glenys Sharpe, for being my scribe and helping me to record my experiences over many years.

Mario Campanale

Mario Campanale has been in my life since I was grown up enough to own my own piano. He could probably number the many years since he first appeared to put my piano and my neighbours out of their misery – but he would be too gallant to do such a thing. His memory, as expressed in this beguiling account of his life, is both phenomenal and affectionate. His childhood, his ever-extending family (a family increasingly composed of friends as well as relatives), is conjured up with humour and delight. Hardships are not glossed over, but encompassed and endured as part of life and life flows on. In describing the Italy of half a century ago he captures not only another country but another era, and throughout his book, though settling in England, he continues his illuminating juxtapositions of differences between cultures, climates and generations. His love of and lifelong involvement with music are a powerful, guiding force, second only to his devotion to Barbara, the independent-minded English girl, whom he met when she was on holiday in Italy. Their travels and travails, trials and triumphs are documented here, but outstanding is the note of abundant generosity and hospitality, allied to the impulse to taste and to celebrate everything that life can offer. After so many years and so many visits from this charming person, it has been a delight to discover and savour some of the sources that have contributed to his great and infectious love of life.

Eleanor Bron

CHAPTER ONE:

Mediterranean Serenade

"My homeland from across the sea is ever calling me…"

Hampton, England July 12th 2006. At the age of seventy years and four days I'm in the middle of a party. The dining room of the Hampton Court Palace Golf Club is decorated with red, white and green, as befits an Italian's celebration.

I am surrounded by friends and family from around the world, all of us gathered together to celebrate both my seventieth birthday and the fact that I have been married to Barbara, the object of my long term holiday romance, for forty five years.

My brother Franco's four piece band is playing. To me he looks little different from the days when we would play in the streets of Cassano, Southern Italy, where we grew up, singing and playing for wages of melons and at the risk of arrest for disturbing the peace.

Champagne is being served on the terrace, not by me – who once served customers in Italian bars and at *The Talk of the Town* – but by waiting staff: I want to tell them that I know what a waiter's life can be.

It is a beautiful sunny evening and we have enjoyed a fabulous buffet with Pugliese wine, what else?

So many loved ones are here with me: our three sons, Anthony, David and Mark, members of our wider family, friends and neighbours – some of whom we have known for all of our married lives. Inevitably, some of those who are most loved can no longer be with us in this life: my mother Alessandra, my father Antonio, my sister Maria and my brother Peppino. And my old friend Conrad Leonard who would spend many hours sitting beside me at the piano transcribing the music I played, turning the melodies into written manuscripts and encouraging me in my song writing.

I still sing. After welcoming everyone tonight I sang two Italian songs and told the story of how Barbara and I met in 1957, our subsequent marriage and our early life in England.

Our friend Maria sang too, continuing the Italian theme. Then Irish music was played on the fiddle, echoing the theme of our many travels not just in Ireland, but around the world.

As Franco and the band began to play, Barbara and I led the dancing – to the theme from *The Godfather*. It seemed appropriate: our neighbours tell us that the family parties we give are reminiscent of scenes from the film.

The music and dancing and laughter will go on long into the night and at the end of it all, we will drive back through Hampton Park in the dark, doing our best to avoid the deer and hoping that the gates have been left open to allow us out.

And then there will be memories and time for reflection. For I have been an Italian in England for nearly fifty years…

Cassano 1947
Mario and the bride!! Age 11

I was born in Cassano Delle Murge –'Cassano of the Hills'- in the south of Italy on 8th July 1936, to Alessandra and Antonio Campanale. I was the fourth of six children: Giuseppe, Rosa, Franco, Mario, Maria and Vincenzo.

My mother was a very small woman – only 4ft 8"- but quick, agile and the brightest and most educated of her family. But my Grandfather was not impressed by girls with ideas above their station, so my mother was expected to work on the land like everybody else, although in her younger days she would escape for a while to the relative ease of a job in the Post Office where she stamped documents with a rubber stamp rather than soil with her boots.

My mother told me that as a child I slept little and lived a lot – nothing much has changed. Once, in desperation, she gave me a large dose of papagna, an extract from poppy seeds: I was one year old. I slept for two days and two nights as a result. My mother was severely reprimanded by my Grandfather who proclaimed with great emotion and Grandfatherly concern: "See what you have done? You have killed your child!" Doubtless he would be amazed to see me now: those poppy seeds did me no harm.

My Mother's medicinal gifts were put to good use in other ways as she was known as Alessandra che fa le iniezioni: 'The Injection Lady'. Somewhere, from someone – we have no idea who – she had learned how to give injections, and even had her own syringe and needles which she sterilised meticulously. Doctors would call on her for help and she would go along to assist them and give whichever injections were needed. Unless it was her own family who needed her skills: she would never let her needle near us and always arranged for 'a professional' to do the deed, if necessary.

My mother was always very attentive to our well being, but strict about our behaviour – the broom was always at hand. When we visited friends and family we were expected to behave. If our behaviour crossed the line we would receive a stern look from her: that one look was enough to stop us.

She would sing as she did the housework, and as the door was usually left open her voice would float out onto the street so that passers by would often slow down to listen – even stop to applaud.

My earliest memories of Cassano are of quiet and freedom. Today it is a busy town of some 8000 inhabitants – a population which swells in the holiday season when apartments, villas and holidays villages offer tourists their Italian Idyll.

But in my childhood it was an agricultural village, surrounded by hills as its name suggests, some of them rising to 1000 feet above sea level. Its inhabitants busied themselves with the harvest of almonds, olives and – because this was, and still is Italy – vineyards.

There was little money and we lived in one large room, divided in two by a curtain. We had no running water or toilet, certainly nothing that could be called 'mod' or 'con'. Yet we were a very happy family and our home, although small, was always filled with passing friends and relatives; the music of animated conversation and the sound of laughter.

We owned two pieces of land which we cultivated, growing broad beans and grain in alternate years, as well as almonds and olives, chick peas, potatoes and rape. The rape we would cook with broccoli and toss in onions and garlic to eat with freshly made pasta: *cavatelli*. It was our favourite dish and always justified two helpings! Once dried, the broad beans would be skinned and cooked slowly as *fave bianche* and served with wild greens or *cicorie*. These were considered the dishes of the poor but have now become something of a speciality – especially amongst vegetarians! The olives were often a sweet variety, fried in oil and salted – and absolutely delicious: Southern Italian cooking at its best – and still available today.

As there were no drains for sewage in the village, a cart drawn by a mule came round every morning to collect our waste. Containers were lifted into the tank and later emptied over the fields where the vegetables were grown.

Despite the fertiliser, we didn't produce enough to feed our family and although my father worked hard on the land, his wage was not enough to keep us. Consequently, as was normal, we were all expected to work to contribute to the family income.

My father was a quiet man who would walk everywhere, often carrying bundles of firewood on his shoulder for miles. He would go without food if times were hard – but never without a cigarette.

He was a proud man, so proud that when his employer was slow to pay his wages he would not ask for them. My Mother would exclaim, "*Se non chiedi per la tua paga, come farò a dare da mangiare ai figli?*" ('If you don't get your wages, how can I feed the children?')

When I was very young my father spent time working in Abyssinia, now Eritrea. It was not a great place for anyone to seek fame and fortune, but when he returned he did bring back some mementoes and small books which we were able to read later. I remember him describing the large bats he saw as 'Vampires of the Forest'.

I also remember him discussing the possibility of war when I was about four or five: mentioning the names of Churchill and Hitler. To me they were just names, but they were uttered with a sense of foreboding and the knowledge of the uncertainty of life.

Once that war began, I would sometimes stand silently at the roadside and watch as German or American soldiers marched past, their boots crunching on the unmade road sending the dust flying. Some would camp outside the village and we would spy on them from a distance daring one another to get ever closer to their forbidden encampment.

We often watched low flying Spitfires somersaulting overhead and would find the fields littered with silver flints which had been spread out to disorientate the radar and which we were told not to touch.

We frequently fled the village because of bombing or earthquakes. Gathering a few possessions together, we would hurry out under the evening sky to spend the night as a family in the relative safety of our shed in the vegetable fields.

One clear, dark night, the British were executing a bombing raid against the Germans in a nearby town when a boat full of ammunition exploded. It was nearly fifteen miles from Cassano and yet we felt the blast and knew its effects for many months afterwards. Franco and I, who were sharing the same bed, were disturbed by a terrific bang. We did little more than sit upright in bed in fear, clutching one another before daring to return to sleep. But when we woke the following morning we were both covered in large spots. They were half an inch in diameter and covered with a hard crust. My mother, ever the apothecary, made a special paste and would spread it over the crust to bring relief to the pain and discomfort. Uncomfortable they may have been – I carry the scars that resulted to this day – but to two small boys, those spots were a blessing in disguise. We were told to miss school for six whole months – although we did have to repeat the school year.

I was a small, dark child with bandy legs, despite being wrapped tightly in sheets with my feet in a bag until the age of 12 months, as was the custom. Despite those legs (which are perfectly straight now, thank you), at the age of four I was sent to a nursery school in the village. It was run by nuns who were very strict, but kind. Every child behaved well as a result. I particularly remember making models with paper or terracotta – something I became very good at.

On some occasions the nursery would stage a play, full of moral exhortation. It included a character who impersonated of the Devil complete with horns, chains to pull at and a three pronged fork. Such hellish horrors were considered perfectly acceptable value-loaded entertainment for pre-schoolers. The lights and sound effects would terrify me. Every flash and bang sent shivers down my spine – but looking back I realise that it was very well done.

One day my father took me to the nursery, my small hand held tightly in his, carefully explaining on the way that my mother wasn't feeling well. Later that day, I heard the church bells tolling and immediately thought that my mother had died. I cried bitterly and would take no comfort from the nuns, despite their best efforts. I was reassured only when my father came to collect me to take me home. Then I could see my Mother – alive and well – for myself, running into her arms to cling tightly to her small but reassuring figure.

We may have had little in terms of material goods, but we were well-loved and secure: I loved it when my father collected me from nursery school on a cold day as he would wrap me snugly inside his cloak for the journey home.

Cassano in the Fifties. Mario was born near the back of the Cathedral in a flat on the right and lived in the little side street on the near left of road.

When Christmas came we would notice that our friends received several toys as presents, whereas we would only get an orange or a bar of soap. When I asked my father the reason for this he explained, often with moist eyes, that he would love to give us presents but that he simply couldn't afford it. As a Father and Grandfather myself, I am now able to appreciate how his generous heart must have ached at such a question. Similarly, I can remember going to school later without the books or pens required because as a family we didn't have the money to buy them. Cruelly, we were slapped by the teacher as a result: although the injustice of such a punishment must have hurt more.

Mussolini was in power by this time – but his antics did little to impact our days. After school, we would wander into the village to various shops, the carpenter or the blacksmith and enjoy helping out.

My musical tendency was already in evidence, as from a very young age I would sing my way through the village with popular songs.

At about eight years old I was given a part-time job in the afternoon following morning school. Franco, aged ten, had already left school and was working for our village photographer so I joined him: homework was confined to the evening.

I was nine when the war ended and Vesuvius erupted although not at exactly the same time. We may have been 150 miles from its site, but the great volcano darkened the sky until late in the morning and left a covering of black ash everywhere. Not wanting to waste anything, the villagers gathered the ash and used it to clean their brass and copper.

The celebrations for Armistice Day were just as explosive and we were treated to fireworks. Somehow the village was not told about the forthcoming celebrations or warned about the rejoicing of friendly gunpowder: when the explosions began, people started to flee the village in fear, fearing attack.

While food was still rationed, we would queue outside the village shops for reconstituted dried milk. Very often the man in charge of the distribution would hit the people in the queue with a stick if they got out of line. He would do well today – ahead of the opening of Harrod's sale.

There wasn't a great variety of food available so our family menus were limited. We ate pulses – mainly dried broad beans- almost every day. On Sunday we would go up a culinary gear and have pasta and ragout with a tiny piece of fatty pork placed on top. Fresh fish from the market was added once or twice a week – sardines, mussels and octopus- as fish was cheap. And in summer we would walk a couple of miles to our own fields where we would pick fresh figs, peaches and plums. When food was short, my Mother and I would dig up a variety of green vegetation from the edges of the field, including dandelions, to supplement our diet.

Every other week, my aunt would make thick, creamy ricotta cheese with its sharp, sour smell. We loved going with a bucket to collect the liquid which was left over from cheese-making to eat with bread. That same aunt would kill a sheep now and again and share the meat with the rest of the family. One day she sent me home with only half of a sheep's head. For some reason she had removed the brains so my mother immediately sent me back to enquire what had happened to the brains and to ask whether it was this particular sheep – or my aunt – who was brainless.

The post-war world may have been changing but age-old customs prevailed.

On one occasion a member of the family suffered a bloodshot eye, the most effective and customary cure for which was new breast milk. A woman who had recently given birth would be found in the village and asked to give the sufferer a few drops of her milk. This was done by the man putting his head in her lap while she expressed a few drops of her milk into his eye. Amazingly, it worked. Although whether it was the delightful experience itself or the milk which cured the man's eye is debatable.

Similarly, it was common for people with a blood disorder to go to the barber-not for a haircut – but so that the barber could apply leeches from a jar to their body. It is easy to understand why, with choice, most men would prefer bloodshot eyes to blood disorders.

We children played in the street: hide and seek, skipping with a rope and hop scotch. We were perfectly safe as there were few cars, the main means of transport being mules and carts: it was easy to outrun a mule to avoid collision.

At around the age of nine or ten we became aware of the differences between boys and girls, and suddenly there were new games to play.

One attractive older girl, Cesarina, would light-heartedly tease me during our street games. On several occasions, in the evenings, she and her friends would ask me to go for a walk to a small village green nearby. It was very dark because there were no street lights, but this suited Cesarina and her friends, for, to my surprise they wanted to kiss and cuddle!

Another girl, Pina, suggested that we should play at weddings. I would be the groom and she would be the bride. This game soon involved more than just the two of us, as her parents and friends made cakes and drinks for the reception and several families became involved in arranging the celebrations. Pina wore a white dress and veil and I wore trousers, a white shirt and sandals. The reception was held in the *forno*, the local public oven where people took their bread and cakes to be baked.

There were about four *forno* in the village where there were huge log fired ovens. Bakery assistants took the dough brought to them by the villagers and pushed it into the ovens with long handled shovels. Strangely, the bakery assistants kept guinea pigs as pets. They were free to run about at will and were accepted as part of the scene. Miraculously, to my knowledge, none were ever baked.

Alongside the guinea pigs and the dough, my childhood wedding took place: the bride blushed, the groom beamed, the reception went well and everyone had a good time. In the evening when I went home and talked about the day's events, my older brother Peppino said, "You should not be here – you should be in your own home since you are married now." For a moment or two I believed him.

As I grew, so did my ambition to become a singer. At school, I was often asked to sing to the class: either the Italian national anthem or Nabucco (considered to be the second National Anthem of Italy) so that the rest of the pupils could learn the tune.

It was customary to have live music to celebrate baptisms, weddings or birthdays, so I would sneak into the receptions from an early age to enjoy listening to the music.

As my voice developed, on occasion, would-be boyfriends of local girls would ask me to sing on their behalf while they mimed. So, late at night, I would stand out of sight under the balcony of the girl in question while the real Romeo stood miming in full view of his beloved. Sometimes this serenading did the trick and true love ran smoothly. On other occasions the romantic music was far from welcome and a neighbour would put an end to the song – and the love- by throwing a bucket of water over the love-struck suitor.

My brother Franco and I were busy in Cassano wherever musical entertainment was needed. If there were special occasions – weddings, birthdays or Christmas parties- the Campanale brothers were there, entertaining the guests.

One evening my brother, myself and his group (a drummer, an accordion player and a guitarist), were asked by a local melon seller to play a serenade at his girlfriend's house. As a reward he said we could help ourselves to as many of his melons as we liked. This was a good deal! So that evening we positioned ourselves near the home of the beauty in question and began singing romantic songs in perfect harmony. Suddenly the door opened and out came her father with a leather belt in his hand-and it wasn't to hold up his trousers. Before we could pack up and leave, or even ask if he had a request, he began lashing out at us resulting in our hurried retreat: a much more difficult feat for the drummer who took the worst of his blows! Despite the brevity of our romantic mission, we helped ourselves to the melons. After all, the songs had been sung-and heard! On another occasion, while playing outside late at night, the *carabinieri* appeared and confiscated our instruments. According to them, we were causing a breach of the peace.

Our part time jobs were a necessity for the family and we often had more than one, even if they weren't always paid well, or at all.

At the age of about nine or ten my mother encouraged me to become a server in our local cathedral. I became the leader of the *crociati* – a group of children the same age as me, who attended the main mass on Sundays. We were to be suitably well behaved and wore a white band with a red cross on our chests. It wasn't all pious solemnity however. On one occasion there was a confirmation at the cathedral with the Archbishop of Bari in attendance. Everything ought to have been well organised so that all would go smoothly. But for some reason, it was a complete shambles: nothing happened when it should have done and all went awry. The Archbishop was so angry that he yelled at the Arch-Priest and the priests to the utter astonishment of the congregation and the half-amused embarrassment of everyone, including the *crociati*.

When Franco left his job with the photographer to work on a nearby farm, I remained. The photographer was known as Pinuccio Giustino, il fotografo, quello che dice sempre; saranno pronte domani le fotografie- the "tomorrow photographer" as he always told his customers that their work would be ready 'tomorrow'. His portfolio was certainly varied. Beyond the usual weddings and portraits he would take photographs of the dead – children included – for the benefit of their relatives. Often the dead person had never been photographed in their lifetime but was eerily 'immortalised' by the camera.

The photographer and his brother did not have a dark room or facilities to develop film behind the shop – and very possibly did not have the skills. Instead they would take the films to be developed in nearby Bari, but neglected to tell me that this fact must be hidden from the customers. One day a customer asked me where the manager was and I innocently told him that he had gone to Bari to have the films developed. A few days later the photographer found out and confronted me. Without any warning he hit me violently on the side of the face, causing me to roll across the room: all this in full view of a customer. He would also send me outside the studio to stand in the street while he was visited by various girlfriends!

As if the many studio duties – and indignities – dealt out by the photographer were not enough, I also had to attend to his pet rabbits and do his shopping. One day I was sent to the fields to pick greens for the rabbits and as I couldn't find exactly what he wanted I returned and told him my predicament. He promptly marched me back to the field and pushed my face into the green vegetables, to show me where they were. He would also leave bank notes spread out on the floor of the studio to see whether I was honest: a trick which eventually led to a row with my mother – and my swift departure from his employment.

Soon after my hasty exit from the photographer's, I began working as a messenger boy at the telephone exchange. By then it was the late forties but the exchange still only had eight subscribers: the town hall, the police station and the odd doctor: it was very quiet.

The telephone was operated by means of batteries and when the batteries were low callers had to shout. I often wondered if telephones were needed for local calls, as I was sure that everyone in the village could hear what was being said without them.

We sometimes received calls arranging for various people to come to the exchange at an appointed time for meetings: often business men who would use the location to sell their produce or secure contracts. One of these men must have been particularly successful in his business dealings as he would offer me 10 lire as a tip to take a message for him.

In time, the telephone exchange became the centre of my own small business empire, as I began to wonder how I could spend the spare time between the very infrequent calls. I decided to learn the craft of basketry. I was a quick learner and was very soon able to make small fruit baskets from cane. I found that hazel shoots worked very well too and at Easter time I made Easter palms from olive branches. When the visitors and businessmen who came to the exchange admired the baskets, I offered to sell them – at quite a profit. My confidence grew, and later, as the managers increasingly left the running of the exchange to me and rarely turned up for work, I put my basketry items on display in the window so that my 'customers' could call in to buy them. The local basket-maker was not too pleased when he found out about my little business.

There were more interesting ways to pass my time at the Telephone Exchange. When I was about twelve, a local family-mainly of daughters – moved into the accommodation above the telephone exchange and began visiting me. In the after-noon, when the parents went for their siesta, one of the sisters began coming into the exchange to talk to me. This eventually led to kissing and cuddling after which she would go back upstairs. The following day another would come down for the same reason. Sometimes the two older sisters would come down together with the same aim – but also to play more innocent games like hide and seek. One day a month, in curious contrast, one of the girls would wear a brown habit with a white cord round the waist: an outward sign that she had been ill and had prayed to St Anthony, who had answered her prayers. I was very glad he had.

When I was 11 years of age I left school and, as if on cue, my aunt and uncle arrived from America. An imposing, prosperous looking man, especially in the environment of Cassano, my Uncle had sought – and found – his fortune in the States. As he got to know me he recognised my artistic aptitude, especially my singing talent, and invited me to go to America, where he felt there would be more opportunities for me. He told me that once he arrived home he would arrange for my cousin Maria Lucia, then aged ten, and I to go to America, as he had, to 'seek fame and fortune'.

It was quite common at that time for people who had left Cassano for the States to return to the village in their big Cadillacs. Some of the men who had divorced, would marry much younger girls from the village and take them back to America. The girls were well aware of the discrepancy in age and the tensions that difference might create. But some even admitted that if things didn't work out they knew they could easily obtain a divorce. They simply seized the opportunity to go to the States to pursue the American dream.

My uncle and aunt returned to America and kept their promise to make arrangements for us to join them: my uncle wanted me to study singing. The necessary papers were produced and sent to Rome and my mother and my aunt followed them to the American Embassy to make the necessary arrangements. They were told that our names would be placed on a waiting list, as there were thousands of hopeful emigrants waiting to be vetted. They were also warned that because we were only related to my uncle through his wife, we had no priority. The dream had to be put on hold: to this day we are still waiting for the outcome.

Our home was in a small cul-de-sac in Cassano, full of closely set houses, their doors and windows overlooking one another. We had no choice but to try to live amicably with our neighbours.

My father's sister and her family lived opposite us and owned the house where we lived – which was next to a bakery. This was wonderful during the winter but almost unbearable in the summer, when the temperature often reached 40 degrees. Then we were forced to take our bedding outside to sleep on the stone pavement underneath the stars.

In addition to our family and my Aunt's, there were four other families living in the street – often they were too close for comfort. When the neighbours opposite spread some gossip about our family, my mother asked the local *carabinieri* for their advice. They told her that they were sorry, but they couldn't intervene unless there was a fight. So my mother decided to give them one. The next time my mother and my sister Rosa met the gossiping neighbour, my tiny but feisty mother grabbed the neighbour's hair and almost shook the life out of her, all the time shouting that she must stop spreading lies about our family. After that brief meeting we somehow didn't have anything to do with our neighbours for a long time. Thankfully the *carabinieri* did not have to be involved.

Living close to our wider family did sometimes have its complications. When my sister Rosa was 14, our cousins lived opposite. Saverio, the eldest son, fell in love with Rosa. They were very discreet about their affection for one another, so no-one guessed for a long time, even though Saverio spent most evenings in our home. When Saverio went into the Army they made a secret promise to marry when he was demobbed. Only when he returned did they at last declare their intentions. As they were cousins there were very strong objections from both families. But their love was so strong that they threatened to run away if consent was not given. My family eventually relented and gave their consent but Saverio's still objected. Rosa and Saverio were eventually married after obtaining permission from Rome, but none of his family attended the wedding, despite the fact that the reception was held in our home, just across the street from theirs.

At the same time, my elder brother Peppino and my youngest cousin, Giuseppina, also fell in love, prompting my worried mother to exclaim, "What are we coming to? Are we going to breed like rabbits?" My brother felt he could not put the family through the same experience twice and subsequently suffered a severe breakdown. As a result Peppino and Giuseppina never married.

While I was still at the Telephone Exchange I was asked if I would help out at the local cinema as a projectionist. I was delighted to accept as I had always wanted the job and went to the cinema at least three or four nights a week. With a job in the cinema I would see every film for free – and as often as I wanted!

It was a tricky job: the projector had a chamber where two carbons had to be kept in line opposite each other but without touching. A constant gap had to be maintained which meant that we had to check every ten minutes. Quite often, one of us who would fall asleep in the heat next to the machine, plunging the cinema into total darkness. The audience, tightly packed into the auditorium would let out a terrific roar, stamping their feet and whistling. While one of us attended to the projector, another had to rewind the spools. Occasionally while we were rewinding the film it would split and we would need to rejoin it with acetone. It was hot, stuffy and often painstaking work, but to keep us happy the owner of the cinema would bring us drinks of wine and beer and freshly char-grilled meat.

At the age of fourteen I closed my basketry business and left the telephone exchange for another change of job which literally took me further afield.

A local entrepreneur- Ciccio Paulo Campanale (no relation) ran a local bus service between both Bari and Cassano and Cassano and Acquaviva. He asked me if I would be a receptionist at the enquiry desk of his central office in Bari, with free bus travel to and fro. So, every morning I would board the bus for the journey to work and listen eagerly to the radio to hear one particular song which had a catchy tune: 'Narcissus' sung by Joyce Grenfell and Norman Wisdom.

After a few months in Bari I was transferred to Acquaviva, where Ciccio Paulo was about to open a new bar, and swiftly appointed as cashier. I was also required to go to the private petrol station to supply the fuel for the bus, and on many occasions had to deputise as a bus conductor, leaving the till to be looked after by a member of the family. Ciccio Paulo had discovered that I was reliable and gave me these responsible positions with confidence. He could see I had potential – and it wasn't long before my bar tending days began.

CHAPTER TWO

"Che vita!" (What a life!)

Ciccio Paulo's new bar in Acquaviva was a popular spot. It had its own small garden which led out to the walkways which meandered under the shade of lines of specially planted trees. It was a regular meeting place for local families and on Sundays everyone would dress in their finery and walk up and down under the trees to be 'seen'.

The bar had large glass windows and a wide frontage onto the street with a good view of everything going on outside.

Inside there was first one long gleaming serving counter followed by another which displayed a range of mouth-watering patisserie. At one end of this counter sat the espresso coffee machine, lauding it over every smaller utensil like a great matriarch. It was here that we made cakes, ice cream and pizza.

As well as serving customers we had the clearing up to do and were constantly wiping, washing, and mopping. We would polish the acres of gleaming chrome, de-mist the mirrors which ran the length of the wall behind the counter and clean the windows that looked out onto the garden and beyond, taking the opportunity to people-spot.

We were constantly 'on the go' rushing from one customer or task to the next, our white cloths neatly folded over our arms and dressed in our white cotton jackets, black trousers, white aprons and bow ties.

Working in the bar was by no means easy. My working hours were from 8 am until midnight when the bar closed, without a single day off. A pastry cook and a barman were also employed, but when there was a shortage of staff all of us had to muck in, making pizzas, *pasticceria* and ice-cream as well as aperitif and coffee.

Every Sunday there was a football match on the green outside the bar which meant we were bursting at the seams with customers. On many occasions I was on my own behind the counter coping with the crowds. My lunch was brought to me by a member of the family but as there was no possibility of a break, I could only look longingly at it from the corner of my busy eye as the food grew cold and inedible.

From my position behind the bar I had a clear view of the game – but it wasn't always a 'good' one. One Sunday the competition was fierce and the crowd grew heated. As a result, the referee was beaten violently by the fans of the losing team. I watched with horror as he was lifted on a stretcher through the heaving crowds and taken to the local hospital. The crowd had attacked him with wooden posts which they had pulled out of the ground, beating him until he became unconscious.

During festivities such as Christmas or Easter, it was common for people in the town to order pastries and cakes from the bar's patisserie. We were expected to work for 48 hours non-stop to fulfil an order, without any extra pay. As no transport was available, we would then face a walk of three miles back to our homes in Cassano.

To make a cake for a wedding was an honour and for one local celebration the pastry cook worked all night to prepare a five tier wedding cake. These works of art were made of layers of sponge cake heavily filled and fully decorated with butter cream or fresh cream. On this particular occasion the cake was to be delivered across the square to the hall of a cinema which had been turned into a reception hall for the wedding: a distance of about 200 yards. The owner of the bar insisted that I help another employee to carry the precious cake across the road. It had been placed on a three legged circular table ready for display-and this was also to be its mode of transport. The two of us looked hopefully at each other, took a deep breath, balanced ourselves either side and lifted the towering culinary masterpiece from the ground, balancing its height nervously between us. Not knowing whether to watch the cake, the road or each other, we began our perilous shuffling from one side of the road to the other in the hope of reaching our destination, our tongues between our lips in intense concentrated effort. But our concentration was interrupted by a familiar sound, and looking up we saw a horse and carriage approaching carrying the bride and her father to the church.

Sadly, taking our eyes off the cake had not been a good move. In our anxiety, one of us – I am honestly not sure which- tripped over one of the table legs. We held our breath for a second that seemed like a month: the cake shuddered, then wobbled and promptly collapsed right in front of the bride. It is hard to say whether she or we were most horrified.

Ciccio Paulo, the bar owner had been watching every step and began shouting at us, saying that we were incompetent good for nothings, while we stood helplessly by. He appealed to the pastry cook as his saviour, urging him to prove his skill by reassembling the cake as fast as possible in time for the reception. He turned from cook to client in turn as he tried to reassure the bride and her father and appeal to the cook in ever more desperate terms.

As the wedding service proceeded we were given the worst duties in the bar, whilst the pastry cook became an architect of heroic renown, rebuilding, moulding and re-decorating the cake, this time in the reception hall. Whether the bride was able to keep her mind off the cake and on her vows, we will never know. But it is easy to imagine the look of relief on her face at the sight of that resurrected tower of sponge and cream.

Our customers were not only a source of occasional hair-raising stress, but of much amusement and entertainment.

A *cancelliere* of the local magistrates court would come into the bar every morning for his coffee. He was an arrogant man with little respect for us, quick to criticise and belittle those he believed were beneath him. The people of Acquaviva would often taunt those from Cassano suggesting that they had their navels on their side. To my annoyance, this man began to address me accordingly: "Hey you who has his navel on his side, make me an espresso!" This went on for several days in front of other customers, until one day I could stand it no longer. To the astonishment of the customers, I unfastened my trousers and dropped them to expose my navel, proving without a doubt that my navel was in the correct place – centre front. The *cancelliere* was aghast at my behaviour and tried to make excuses, saying that his comments were meant as a joke. Far from getting me into trouble, he never again suggested that my navel – or anything else – was anywhere other than where it should be.

Another customer, a local judge known for his parsimonious streak would cheat us out of the normal minimum five lire tip by placing five lire on the plate and taking two lire back – although, unlike the *cancelliere*, he was, at least, kind and polite.

Don Ciccio Pepe was the secretary of the local hospital and extremely finicky about hygiene, so much so that he would not accept well used bank notes in his change. Every time he touched the notes he would disinfect his fingers with spirit which he carried around with him, and if he accidentally dropped a packet of cigarettes on the floor he would not pick it up. When ordering his very small espresso coffee he would make sure that we disinfected the cup thoroughly under the steamer and would wash its rim while stirring his coffee, presumably to make absolutely sure that the cup was sterilised. Another customer we nicknamed "*poco zucchero*" because he would always ask for coffee with 'a little sugar'.

When I was about fifteen, one of the customers, Sig. Cafaro, offered me a job working for him as an assistant technician. He had a showroom at the bottom of the square from which he sold Singer and Necchi sewing machines and gas hobs. He and his wife lived in a flat above the shop and offered me accommodation. This seemed an improvement on the long hours in the bar, so I accepted his invitation.

Sig. Cafaro's wife, Sig.ra Lina, came from a well respected and wealthy family of landowners, and as they were unsure of my table manners I was at first asked to eat in the kitchen by myself, while they ate in the dining room. After three months I was passed fit for politeness – and they invited me to take my meals with them. However, when the elderly lady who cooked and cleaned stopped working for them, I was expected to add her duties to mine: washing and waxing the floors, cooking meals and washing up – hardly the duties of a sewing machine technician! Sig. Cafaro also supplied his customers with large gas cylinders for cooking and it was my job to take the cylinders to the customers' homes – by bicycle. This exercise required the skills of a circus performer and the strength of a Strong Man. That I managed such a pedalling and balancing feat is still a source of amazement to me.

One day I was sent to the obsessively hygienic, coffee-cup wiping, Don Ciccio's home to balance and deliver my canisters. To my surprise, I found that Don Ciccio's kitchen was absolutely filthy. I could only imagine that he had his meals served in the dining room by his wife and had never set foot in his own kitchen!

I stayed with the Cafaro family for over a year during which time I discovered that Sig. Cafaro had an uncontrollable, and at times, terrifying temper which he vented on anybody within range – including his wife and I. He would rant on and on in an explosion to merit any which might result from his gas canisters and no one was allowed to speak until he calmed down.

One day, I was invited, along with Sig.Cafaro, for a pre-nuptial celebration at the house of a friend. About ten of us enjoyed a typical Italian lunch, toasted the happy couple with plentiful supplies of local wine and generally enjoyed one another's company. At the end of the meal Sig. Cafaro told the hosts that as I was so good at washing up I would tackle the ensuing debris for them. In other words I was 'ordered' to wash up, which as a guest I resented. But I wanted to avoid the characteristic Cafaro explosion in the company of friends especially on such a happy occasion so I obliged. The following day I told Sig. Cafaro that I had to go home to see my family. On hearing my story, my mother was outraged at my treatment and we decided that I should leave Sig.Cafaro's employment for good.

Some time later Sig. And Sig.ra Cafaro Cafaro led me to believe that if I stayed with them they would adopt me and eventually inherit their wealth. But their promises seemed rather vague!

Just a few days later I found a new job in Acquaviva in another bar. My new employers were Sig. And Sig.ra Capozzi. They were strict, meticulous and very keen on cleanliness. Sig.ra Capozzi always made sure that there was a place for everything and that everything was in its place – including me. His hair and moustache were neatly combed so that he resembled Clark Gable.

To begin with I travelled to work by bus, leaving early in the morning and arriving home late in the evening. After a few months it was suggested that I should sleep at the Capozzi home, which I did, although this inevitably meant that I worked longer hours. The new arrangement worked fairly well when the weather was cool but during the summer when the temperature rose it was unbearable. The room I slept in was unventilated and the small bed was too soft for comfort and sank in the middle. I would sleep badly and dream heavily, tossing and turning, and would wake up having dreamt that I was swimming as the bedclothes were soaked with sweat.

In the hot weather, Sig. Capozzi and I would deliver ice cream to customers on a Vespa motor scooter. Whilst this was an easy exercise after the rigours of gas canisters on bicycles, it still required some considerable skill – and the strong desire for a cool breeze. I would cling on to Sig.Capozzi with my right hand while, with my left hand I held a tray of up to 20 glasses full of ice-cream high above my head. The warm air inevitably meant that the ice cream would begin to melt resulting in a less than appetising presentation on delivery.

I didn't stay very long with the Capozzi family because of the working and sleeping conditions, but when I left I was immediately offered another job with a family called Gentile, at Bar Commercio also in Acquaviva. My association with the Gentile family would turn out to be a much longer one with much more to worry about than melting ice cream.

Sig. Gentile was given a nickname by the townspeople: *'fascid'* meaning spark, as he too had an explosive temperament. His real name was Vito and his wife was

Angela Benemerito. Vito was a shrewd operator with a finger in a number of business pies who cleverly registered the business in his wife's name for tax purposes.

Vito and Angela had five daughters and one son, and despite his sparky temperament, Vito also had a lover by whom he had two more sons. Vito started as he meant to go on, and the very first morning I began working for him he gave me a flask of freshly made espresso coffee which I had to deliver by bicycle to his lady-love.

The Gentile daughters were also a combined force to be reckoned with. The eldest was Cecilia, and then there was Zenobia. The girls were punctuated by Luigi the son; then came Maria Francesca and finally the youngest, whose name has disappeared from my memory – probably under the shadow of her sisters. Maria and Francesca were boarders in the local convent, although I would soon discover that this education had done little for their morals!

Vito soon discovered that I was trustworthy and as I often had to pay large sums of money into the bank on his behalf, he made me imitate his signature so that I was able to do all his financial transactions for him. He was very pleased with the way I ran the bar saying, "Anything you do is OK with me, Mario." He wouldn't always feel that way, however.

His wife Angela was illiterate, but very astute and brilliant at mental arithmetic. She was no beauty either, but was very sexually seductive to men simply by clever use of her body language. Her lover was proof in point. He was an influential gentleman by the name of Silvio Cirielli, a prominent and successful town councillor who later became senator. He was also the Gentile's *consigliere*: the family financial and business advisor.

Angela and Silvio Cirielli went to great lengths to hide their affair from me, especially in the evenings when I was left on my own in the bar. They would often stage fake arguments in an attempt to throw me off the scent. I would hear them quietly say to one another: "Don't worry about Mario, he doesn't understand" when I understood only too well. First, Silvio would leave the bar, and then Maria (Angela's sister) would join me behind the counter and ask me to fetch something from somewhere else in the building. Upon my return Angela would have gone, having disappeared into the kitchen at the back of the bar, locking the door behind her. Silvio would then enter through the back door so that they were able to be alone. Meanwhile Maria would take advantage of her sister's absence – and mine – to help herself to money from the cash drawer. I would sometimes sneak out around the back of the building to peep through the keyhole of the kitchen door, where the interesting sights confirmed my suspicions.

One evening when Angela and Silvio were in the kitchen being interesting together, I went outside the bar to clear up and saw Vito, Angela's husband, returning from his own lover's house. I was terrified that he would go inside and catch the two lovers in the heat of their kitchen. Instead, pre-occupied with his own obvious infidelity, Vito came towards me with a look of mild panic on his face. "You haven't seen me" he said and promptly hurried on his way home.

Although Vito and Angela knew of each other's lovers they never spoke of them. It was inevitable, however, that at some point their pot of double deceit would boil over. One day there was a lively argument during which Vito grabbed his wife by her hair, shaking her violently whilst screaming abuse. Later in the day their tempers cooled as each had realised that it was in both their interests to accept the status quo. Although Vito disliked the relationship between his wife and Silvio Cirielli, he had to put up with it: as a town councillor with influence and contacts, Silvio was extremely useful to him as an adviser and for passing business his way.

Vito supplied fruit and vegetables to the local hospital and always prepared the boxes by putting the best fruit at the top to make them look attractive, hiding the far from perfect pieces underneath. I would be sent to deliver the fruit, pushing a handcart through the streets to the hospital. Once the nun who was in charge of the hospital catering noticed what was going on, it was inevitable that I would be the one to get the blame for Vito's sneaky scam.

Vito's dishonesty extended to his employees as well as his customers. It was important that he collect the necessary stamps on my insurance card in case of my injury, but Vito considered this unnecessary. He told me that if I was hurt and had to go to hospital he had friends there who would look after me. (I could only think of the angry, foiled-by-fruit nun.) On the occasions when the government inspector came round to check on employees, I was told to 'disappear' so that Vito could avoid paying my insurance. Some years later, when I was in the army, I was still troubled by the fact that Vito had not made those insurance payments. As I didn't want him to get away with it I wrote a private letter to Silvio Cirielli demanding that he should advise the family to cover my stamps for the period I worked there. Although I knew enough about Silvio's various relationships with the family to sink him, I made it clear that I was not interested in blackmail, but simply requesting my entitlement. I discovered later that the Gentile family had only covered two years of insurance out of the six years I had worked for them.

As Bar Commercio was right in the centre of the large square in Acquaviva it was a popular venue for meetings.

The town's blacksmith was a brother of Sig. Cafaro my former employer (the third brother was a bishop in a nearby town). He was also the elected mayor of Acquaviva. One day he came into the bar with his entourage – including his brother, my previous boss. They took their seats at several adjoining tables, deep in conversation, and I approached them, as was the custom, to ask what they would like to drink. The mayor turned to me and snapped: "Who called you?" To which I boldly replied, "Sir, it is my duty to come and ask what you wish to drink when you arrive in the bar." The mayor, equally taken aback and impressed by my reply suddenly said "Bravo!" At which point his brother saw an opportunity for some credit at my expense and said, much to my indignation, "See how I've brought up this young man?"

One day we heard that a Mafia leader had just arrived in town. He had been exiled from Castellammare di Stabia, a town in the south of Naples – where the

Mafia was called *'Camorra"* – after assaulting a Member of Parliament. He started to frequent the Bar Commercio, where he soon made friends with the local people, frequently offering drinks to everyone – he also gave good tips. In my naivety, I was surprised that he was a Mafia boss because he seemed such a gentleman, polite and courteous. Once a week he would be visited by his entire family who travelled from Naples for emotional reunions. After befriending both him and his family I found out where they lived in Castellammore di Stabia and a few years later – still naïve – decided to visit them while I was in Naples. I found the address and pulled at the bell, but when the door was answered it was made very clear to me that the family didn't want to know me: a 'gentleman' he may have been – but he was still *'camorra".*

Before long the Gentile family suggested that I lodge with them and share their meals, which I did – although the privileges of a lodger stopped there. One of the girls, Zenobia, did all the cooking, cleaning and washing, but as that didn't include my washing and I wasn't allowed to use their bath, I had to return home each time I needed a bath or a change of clothes. I might have gone home by public transport but Vito, worried in case I didn't return, insisted on taking me home and back by car. He would sit outside in his car while I had my bath, periodically and anxiously peering at the house until I was ready to go back with him.

One Easter, after working for 48 hours without a break, I asked if I could go home on Easter Monday to see my family. Vito reluctantly agreed, telling me to be back as soon as possible. I travelled to Cassano by bus to find the whole family gathered together, including my Aunt and Uncle from Bari. They all decided to go for a walk to the nearby convent, as was the tradition. My Aunt insisted on my not going back to work that afternoon, so that I could go with them – it was Easter after all. When Vito realised I had not returned he set out to look for me and found us amongst the crowds walking towards the convent. He reprimanded me in front of my relatives, saying I had broken my word. I had no choice but to go back with him, but not before my Aunt had very publicly given him a piece of her mind about my long working hours and his suitability as an employer for her nephew!

Every time my wages were due, Vito would say "It's nothing to do with me; you will have to ask my wife." Then she would say the same thing: "Go to my husband". My wages were always paid late, even though I would notice Vito's free and frequent production of a large roll of bank notes from his pocket.

As I now lodged at his home, he would send someone to knock at the door and wake me up at 8 o'clock in the morning – whatever time I had got to bed the night before. He always opened the bar at 5 a.m., mainly for the benefit of the land workers who would call in for coffee before going to work. I would take over from him at 8.30 a.m. And work till at least midnight – a very long day – with very short meal breaks. He would often treat me as if I was stupid, giving me café latte made with diluted coffee as soon as I arrived, failing to realise that I could easily make myself the best coffee in town, once he had left.

One of the nuns from the convent, Sister Giovanna, came to the bar frequently to talk to the girls' family. It was rare enough for women to be seen in the bar, but a nun in full habit was quite a sight! She would stand by the counter talking to the men who were gathered there – including the famous Don Ciccio – and thoroughly enjoy herself.

Sister Giovanna's lessons on piety and chastity must have fallen on deaf ears as far as the Gentile girls were concerned. Some time later I discovered that the two girls, who stayed at the convent, knew far more about the facts of life than I did. When Maria was sixteen, she left the convent and returned to live with her family. One afternoon she had to return to her home nearby for some reason and asked me to give her a piggy back ride. When I reluctantly agreed she jumped on my back and to my astonishment rubbed herself up and down until she was sexually aroused!

During the winter months when there was less work in the bar I would be sent back to the Gentile family home in the middle of the day to rest at the same time as the family. Luigi would go to bed and so would Maria and Zenobia. Zenobia slept on her own in a bed in a recess, while Maria slept under the stairs sharing a bed with her older sister, Cecilia. As I was not tired enough to sleep I would play the accordion and sing songs.

I began to be attracted to Maria and she knew it. During the day, when she was working, Maria would be at the cash desk and noticing my attention would flirt with other men to make me feel jealous. Her favourite flirting partner was a man called Gigino who often came into the bar for a drink. I couldn't stand his arrogance and he was often rude to me. One day, as I was operating the espresso machine, I was so distracted by watching them across the bar that I did not realise that I was pushing the precious machine off the edge of the counter. Luckily, I noticed just in time. Gigino belonged to a group of young men who went about enjoying themselves, in the mode of the film La Dolce Vita, which was very popular at the time. He had a cousin called Gianni Ross, who was tall, good looking and well educated. Gianni had spent most of his life in Milan until the family came back to live in Acquaviva. Cecilia, the eldest sister, was an attractive, typically southern Italian girl with dark curly hair and would come in every day to take over behind the bar to give us a break. If she was working when Gianni came in she would do anything to attract his attention – even unbuttoning the top of her blouse. She was also very superstitious and her great desire was that her first child should be a boy. So, according to superstition she made sure that whatever she ate was counted out in odd numbers – three grapes, five nuts – in the belief that this would ensure a male heir. In the course of time she got her man, eventually marrying Gianni. But I found out later that her first child was a girl and that she had not been able to show her the affection that she was able to give to her second child, a boy.

When Vito, ever the shrewd businessman, found out that Cecilia was going to be married he made sure that he got his wife Angela pregnant, as at that time Italian law stated that families with six children were exempt from higher taxes. Perfectly to plan, the baby was born at around the time that Cecilia and Gianni were married.

Vito's ruthless shrewdness extended beyond the crust of many a business pie. He was a partner in the local cinema – the Cosmo – situated in the middle of the square. He would go to watch the latest films for free whenever he wanted and afterwards would come into the bar and tell us the whole story, saying "Now I've told you the story you don't need to go to see the film.' Why his business brain didn't extend to realising that this would deter us from going and lose him revenue, I can't imagine.

Never one to miss a business opportunity, Vito installed an enormous container in a large room at the back of the bar in which to make ice. The ice was sold to ice cream makers or for butchers to use in their chiller cabinets and was invaluable for making *gelato* or for keeping meat cool. Ice making was heavy, difficult work. It meant lifting a huge container full of salted water into which a main metal liner would be positioned to be filled with water which would freeze. The containers were about four feet deep, and I had to climb on top of the counter to insert the metal liner. The day after freezing, in order to remove the ice that had formed, I would need to lift the metal liner out and carry it to a large tub full of warm water which would melt the ice inside enough for it to be removed. I would then carry the enormous blocks of ice, weighing about 30 or 40 pounds each, to a chiller cabinet. There they would finally be carefully arranged ready for collection by the butchers and ice cream vendors. It was backbreaking, heavy and dangerous work.

Minor accidents were common in the course of a working day. I frequently cut my fingers, which would often turn septic. Vito would send me off to the local hospital where I would arrive in some trepidation. The doctor would often need to cut the swelling to remove the septic poison and then apply a strong antiseptic. Sometimes I would faint and he would wave smelling salts under my nose to waken me. Needless to say, I went straight back to work afterwards.

Once a month the bar staff were expected to stay after bar closing hours so that the area behind the counter could be thoroughly cleaned. We often didn't leave until three o'clock in the morning after an exhausting day.

When there were weddings we prepared cassata Ice creams for up to 400 people, beginning the preparations two or three days beforehand and continuing after the bar was closed. Once the ice-cream making process was started it had to be continued until the ice cream was completed, so once again we didn't get to bed until 3 am.

On other occasions, Angela would wake up during the night thinking that the espresso machine in the bar had not been switched off at the end of the evening. Because the machine didn't have a safety valve, it would explode if it reached a very high pressure (much like Vito). Anxiously roused from my sleep, I would be required to accompany Angela back to the bar in the darkness to check that everything was in order. Inevitably it always was, but I often had nightmares about that machine exploding.

As far as I knew, Vito had no sisters or brothers, but Angela had two of each. The younger sister, Concetta, was a very attractive girl who eventually married 'La Dolce

Vita's Gigino to my disgust: I thought she deserved someone better. Her family doubtless encouraged the match because Gigino had a regular job at the town hall which was secure – and also because he was a friend of Silvio's.

Angela's younger brother was an ice cream vendor: an arrogant, swearing, bully- and lazy with it. As he got up so late in the mornings, he started his working day late and always grumpily demanded immediate service from me when he came in each day for his ice blocks.

Life in the bar was a hard life for one so young. At weekends, all my contemporaries would be gathered in the square outside, dressed up in their best clothes, laughing and trying to impress the groups of girls who would stare at them shyly, giggling from the sidelines, or plan ways to attract their attention. I would watch them through the window as I wiped the bar top and made coffee, and envy their freedom, resenting the fact that I had to work. To make matters worse, my willingness to do everything asked of me in the bar meant that the family teased me, calling me "half a woman". In order to prove them wrong I paid a great deal of attention to Maria and Zenobia!

The Gentile family's demands on me were forever increasing, and in my tiredness, I started accidentally breaking things. One summer afternoon, as I was adjusting the glass topped tables on the patio outside, one of the tables fell and the glass broke. Something inside me finally snapped in a similar way and I walked away from the bar, apron and all. I walked through the town at an increasing pace, out into the countryside, just wanting to put distance between myself and the Bar Commercio. I padded onwards towards Bari, an odd figure with my anxious brow, my hurried step and my white flapping apron, hiding myself like a fugitive whenever a car approached. Eventually, I arrived at a town called Adelfia. It was late afternoon and a group of saddlers were working outside their shop. By strange coincidence one of the men's mothers was my Godmother, he recognised me and we entered into conversation. He realised that I had run away from my work and felt concerned both for me and for those who might be worried. So without telling me, he sent someone to telephone the bar in Acquaviva, and my family, to let them know where I was. Eventually Vito arrived to collect me. He was silent and stern but there were no explosions. After thanking the people of Adelfia for looking after me he drove me back to Cassano, questioning me, receiving little response in return and repeating his warnings about the terrible things that befall bar workers who go astray. When we arrived in Cassano all my family were gathered anxiously waiting to see me, relieved that I was safe. In a calmer moment I explained to Vito why I had run away. Amazingly, he listened: from then on the Gentile family became less demanding and I had a little more time off.

But my escape from the bar had been a turning point, and I began to allow myself to dream a little.

CHAPTER THREE

L' alba (The Dawn)

Flat feet did not make me exempt. At 18, to my surprise, I passed my National Service medical examination: suddenly I knew that change was ahead. By Italian law at that time everybody was required to do eighteen months National Service unless they were exempt on medical grounds. My elder brother Peppino had been given exemption with flat feet. As mine were flat too, I had hoped for the same exemption – but Peppino's feet were obviously flatter!

As I waited for 'call up', moving my attention from my feet to my voice seemed the best course of action.

It was still my ambition to sing, so whenever there was a wedding reception at the Cosmo cinema I would usually be on stage singing with the band. My great ambition, however, was to sing in English. The Gentile family teased me, not only for singing but for my specific wish to sing in a foreign tongue, "But you won't understand what you're singing about!" they taunted.

Few people had TV sets in their homes, so they would go to bars where large sets were prominently placed. Vito, with an eye on the business benefits, made sure the Bar Commercio was no exception. The seating was arranged in rows like a cinema, creating very good business. By watching the television placed in the bar, I avidly followed the Festival of Italian Song held in San Remo every year.

Following music festivals meant that I also got to know the names of popular entertainers and singers of the time, one of whom – Nilla Pizzi – was considered the Vera Lynn of Italy. I regularly bought a music magazine and would be found poring over the photographs of my idols and reading about their performances and their lifestyles.

Early in 1956, just before my 20th birthday, I noticed an advert for a national singing competition which was to be held in Cattolica, near Rimini: Nilla Pizzi was to join the panel of judges. When I expressed my wish to take part in this competition, the Gentile family were determined to put me off: "You would only be good enough to clean Nilla Pizzi's shoes" they quipped, laughing uproariously at their own suggestion. Of course, this only made me more determined to enter and I began saving for my train journey to Cattolica with my mother's encouragement, at least.

On the 10th July, my fare saved, and leaving the Gentile family open-mouthed at my determination, I travelled to Rimini, near Cattolica, in order to take part in the singing contest. The competition was such a huge event in comparison to the brevity of my appearances that there seemed very little to it – except a great deal of waiting. So while I waited, I went visiting.

My elder brother Peppino, who had a barber's shop in Cassano, suggested that I should visit the Antonio Casamassima family as Antonio was stationed in Rimini in the *carabinieri* force. Antonio's wife, Anna, had two brothers: Enzo, a doctor who also ran the family business, and Gastone.

I discovered that the family were about to open a new bar in Rimini – Bar Clipper – so I asked if they required any more staff. Sig.ra Quinta, Anna's mother, said that she was very sorry but they had all the staff they needed. There certainly seemed to be enough: Mario Giovannini was in charge of the bar, there was an ice-

Rimini in the fifties

cream maker who also had to be the waiter, a bar assistant and members of the family. I explained that I quite understood, but promised that the following morning, at the official bar opening, I would sit in a corner of the bar and wait: "If you need me I will be there to help" I said, "but if not I'll go back to Cattolica and go home after the competition."

The next morning, I sat in my corner for a mere fifteen minutes before the bar became so busy that Sig.ra Quinta called across to me "Sig. Mario, please put your white jacket on, we need you!" I leapt to my feet and joined the busy bar staff, and as there was another Mario working at the counter, I was quickly nicknamed 'Mariolino'.

The following day I went back to Cattolica to sing my second piece in the competition and later heard that I had just missed gaining a place as a semi-finalist, coming 11th out of 600 contestants. The news was both a disappointment and an encouragement. I really could sing!

To my delight Sig.ra Quinta asked me to stay on at Bar Clipper for the rest of the season. Dr Enzo fixed my pay at 1,500 lire per day basic, plus accommodation and food, just to help behind the counter. I was told that when I had to serve at the tables outside I would receive 18% of the group takings, plus tips. I could hardly believe their generosity and was overwhelmed. A few weeks later, after Enzo had taken some business advice from an expert in bar management, he told me that he was very sorry but he

Mario and Gastone

had made a mistake with my wages – but still proposed that I should receive 14% of the takings. I readily agreed as this was still a very good proposition – I only wished he could introduce his 'expert in bar management' to the Gentile family.

During that summer season of 1956 working in Bar Clipper, I started to learn about the foreigners who came to Rimini on holiday.

I particularly noticed the eccentric way the English people dressed, especially the men. Their holiday attire consisted of long trousers rolled up at the ankle, a singlet, heavy sandals and a white handkerchief worn on their heads and knotted at the four corners: hardly the understated English style I had always imagined. They wandered along the streets oblivious of the spectacle they made. Yet, despite their lack of fashion sense, the English tourists were the most generous with tips and would often come into the bar at the end of their holiday to leave a tip with me personally.

Before long I would find myself able to distinguish between different nationalities, not only through their language, but by their unique characteristics, and could quickly tell whether they were French, English Scandinavian, Swiss or German.

One evening an enormous German woman, apparently straight from a Wagner opera, came into the bar with her husband, both of them half-drunk. She put a record on the juke box and loudly and amorously insisted that I dance with her, grabbing my arm and pulling me towards her. Because of the difference in our height my face ended up right between her ample breasts. As she squeezed me closer to her I felt as if I was suffocating!

As my desire to sing was so strong – even if not at that particular suffocating moment – my employers warmly encouraged me to sing and play my guitar to the customers late at night. Customers enjoyed my singing and it was a way of encouraging them to linger longer.

One evening two men and a girl came in. They had formed a group which moved from bar to bar, and would sing and play their guitars with the benefit of an amplifier and microphone. As all the tables outside were occupied and my waiting skills weren't needed for a while, I was encouraged to join in with them and sing outside using the group's microphone. The passing traffic gradually came to a standstill as an enormous crowd gathered to listen to us. While I was singing the girl in the group seized the opportunity to collect money from the listening crowd to share amongst us. It was great fun and the resulting bar business went down well with my employers. But the bar across the road was deserted, its owner scowling out at us through his empty windows. The following morning I was genuinely afraid that he would cross the road with the single intention of putting a stop to my impromptu entertainment for good.

While working at Bar Clipper, I befriended a local photographer. By coincidence he knew Nilla Pizzi – my singing idol – very well and told me all about her. As I was so keen to meet her, he arranged for me to do just that and organised a meeting on the beach where he promised I could have my photograph taken with her. In my excitement I thought little of what I should wear and turned up excitedly at the specified time to find Nilla Pizzi in a swimming costume. As I had no swimming trunks I had to roll up my trousers, to my shame, in the English fashion. When I returned to the Gentile family at the end of the season, and showed them the photograph of "Me with Nilla Pizzi on the beach" they could scarcely believe their eyes. I was far from cleaning her shoes, as they'd anticipated. In fact, neither of us was wearing any!

That summer season in the Rimini bar was a very exciting time. Work was well paid and enjoyable; I felt appreciated by my employers; I had plenty of opportunities to sing – and I was meeting people from all over Europe.

Groups of English customers who knew about my love of singing would ask me to join in with their sing-songs. One group especially liked the "Banana Boat Song" made popular by Harry Belafonte, so, at last, I learnt the English words to a song. I sang the verse solo while the customers became my backing group.

Rimini, Summer 1956.
Mario with Nilla Pizzi

On another occasion a Swiss couple who had been drinking in the bar found that they had both left their money in their hotel and couldn't pay the bill. So the husband left his wife in the bar as security while he went back to the hotel for his wallet. To the mock dismay of his wife and our great amusement, he left the bar running with his arms outstretched as if about to fly away!

Coach tour hostesses regularly came into the bar and one invited me to join her party as her guest on a day excursion to Venice. The bar was very busy, but this was an opportunity I knew I couldn't refuse. Thankfully, my employers gave me permission, and a few days later I left early to join a coach full of English tourists – destination Venice. En route we visited Ravenna and Padua finally arriving in Venice to visit palaces, churches and restaurants and took a gondola ride, all of which was entirely free-at least to me! To spend the whole day simply enjoying myself with no thought of work was a rare treat and there was something special about seeing some of the most the significant sights of my own country for the first time through the eyes of others.

We left to travel back to Rimini at about eight in the evening, tired and happy. I was encouraged to sing for everyone on the coach, concluding what was, at that point, the most wonderful day of my life.

Sandstorms and thunderstorms often hit Rimini with little warning. We would have to move fast at the first sign of either: battening down the high shutters of the bar and taking as many tables and chairs inside as possible. Business would come to

Cassano 1957.
FROM LEFT: **Cousin Carlo-Franco, Peppino & Mario**

a standstill as guests wouldn't even begin to venture outside their hotels. We would be left in the bar doing odd jobs, looking hopefully at the skies and waiting. But the pace soon quickened once the storm had passed, when the trick was to replace the tables and chairs as fast as possible to beat the competition.

One summer morning, as I was waiting for customers, I noticed four beautiful, tall, German girls in bikinis strolling towards the bar. On impulse I pretended to faint and fell to the ground, dropping my tray, to the consternation of the girls and the intense amusement of Mario Giovannini behind the bar. I 'came round', looked up into the faces of the girls who were desperately trying to revive me, and promptly pretended to faint again. When I eventually got up and the girls were sure I was fully recovered, they decided to stay and have a cappuccino! My boss was delighted by my little ruse.

After a successful and happy summer season at Bar Clipper, I reluctantly returned to Cassano and began looking for a job. As soon as the Gentile family found out that I had returned, they asked me to go and work for them. I had little choice – but at least I had that photograph!

Neapolitan songs were becoming very popular at that time, so after a few months back with the Gentile family at Bar Commercio, I decided to go to Naples to have singing lessons and to learn the Neapolitan language – which is completely different from Italian. It was the next step towards my dream.

Luckily, I was told by a member of the family that a man from Cassano, Sr. Paciolla, a Master Sergeant in the Italian Air force, was stationed at Naples airport: I would have a contact.

I left for Naples late in December 1956, to the annoyance of the Gentile family, and found accommodation through a man from Cassano-Tonino, brother in law of Ciccio Paolo who travelled to Naples regularly on business.

Naples had an enormous impact upon me. As a city, it was much larger than Bari, bustling and lively. The traffic was chaotic: cars meandered across squares and squeezed through back alleys against the odds; pedestrians were shooed noisily out of the way and the sound of car horns added a distinctive rhythm to the sound of the city.

The main streets hid a maze of tiny alleyways like the workings behind a clock-face. The tall, ancient buildings were linked across alleyways with criss-crossed washing lines tied between their balconies. Heavy bed-sheets and assorted laundry were strung across from building to building like giant flags in celebration – a celebration of ordinary life. From the alleyway beneath it was just possible to catch a glimpse of blue sky, high above the canopy of laundry. Small children ran in and out of doorways chased by harassed mothers who whipped at them with cloths and raised their arms in exclamation at their antics. Women called to one another across balconies, arguing the point or laughing at the stories their men had told to explain their absences of the night before. Everywhere there were signs of life, hectic busyness and energy. Even at night it seemed as if Naples was a city which never slept. It was a far cry from sleepy Cassano.

My lodgings were in the home of the Borrelli family who lived near the centre of Naples in an area called Galascione. My small room was situated above an archway leading to the waterside and in order to get to street level I had to go up, either in a lift or via a flight of steep steps.

As soon as I was settled, I contacted the Master Sergeant, who invited me to his home to meet his

Torre Canne Beach 1958.
Peppino enjoying a drop of wine!!

family. Sr. Paciolla listened carefully as I shared my ambition to sing. Something in my words must have made my ambition infectious, because he immediately decided that he would take a day off work to help me to look for a job.

Once in the city centre we walked from one end of the street – Via Roma – to the other. We ended up near the sea in the Margellina district in a small square called Piazza del-Martiri. There we found a very elegant bar called the Bar Cristallo. The manager was Milanese and ran the bar in a very business-like manner. Once he found out that I was not Neapolitan, he employed me straight away. Neapolitans, he said, were considered unreliable. I soon discovered that most of the staff were Neapolitan – and far from unreliable.

I began work at the Bar Cristallo immediately and soon became acquainted with its wealthy and influential customers.

The tea room at Bar Cristallo was very elegant: its high ceilings hung with twirling fans to alleviate the oppressive Naples heat. It was spacious, tastefully furnished and very much the place to be seen, with a cocktail bar adjoining the tea room. A specialist ice cream maker came every morning to make fresh ice cream using the best ingredients, while afternoon tea was a very grand affair. Silver tea pots and the finest crockery would be carried across the room at the request of the socialites of Naples who would come in almost every afternoon to drink tea and eat delicate pastries. The ladies would gather in furs and hats, modelling the latest fashions. They would appear inside the door and stand just for a few seconds to ensure that they had been noticed, before walking elegantly to their tables to greet their friends and acquaintances, remove their gloves and sip their tea or share the latest gossip. The air would be filled with the murmur of urgent conversation and the chinking of the best bone china.

One day Sig.Lauro, a well known shipping magnate, came into the cocktail bar. He was an impressive figure, well fed and expensively dressed in a well cut suit, his silk tie just so. His presence alone sent a commanding message. He ordered some cocktails and, as is the Italian custom, paid for them first leaving a very small tip, a single coin. The barman, offended, deliberately rolled the coin so that it fell on the floor and landed by Sig.Lauro's foot. To the disgust of the barman, Sig. Lauro simply glanced at it and promptly carried on talking to his friends. The offence he gave to others was of no concern to him.

Every barman had his own duties in the bar Cristallo. We worked eight hour days and were paid regularly on time every Friday – a practice that was still a delightful novelty to me. Our shifts were staggered so that we worked on three days from the morning until the afternoon and on the other four days from the afternoon until midnight. It was a good system and an arrangement which allowed me, at last, to take singing lessons – with Maestro Giannini.

Giannini was a conductor, composer and arranger who conducted the band for Radio Naples. He had also launched the careers of several Neapolitan singers: Mario Abbate; Giacomo Rondinella and Pina Lamara. I hoped that Mario Campanale would be next on his list.

My daily routine was quickly established and revolved around work, singing lessons and new friends. Life was fast and fresh and interesting. Even the walk to work was eventful.

The buildings in the street where I stayed were several storeys high and filled with families. I found it amusing to watch the ladies come out onto their balconies in the morning when the vendors came selling their wares. They would stand in the street below and shout up to the ladies to attract their attention and secure their custom. Once alerted and engaged, the ladies would lower their baskets to the ground. The vendor would place the goods inside and the baskets would be pulled perilously skyward again, disappearing into a window or balcony: a basket of lemons perhaps, some household cleaning item or olive oil. If everything was satisfactory, the money would be placed in the basket and lowered down for a final time. If it wasn't satisfactory anything could happen – from a shout of disgust to the hurried descent of reject goods. While all this was going on, gentlemen on their way to work would greet the ladies and lift their hats saying, "Good morning Donna Caterina"; " Good Morning Donna Maria", and so on all the way down the street, like an early morning chorus.

I soon discovered that there was a short cut from my lodgings to work which took me across a yard belonging to an elderly woman. She would see me step into her courtyard before I knew I was there myself and would be ready to meet me, arms folded, feet apart and ready for combat. She must have owned one of the most enterprising business brains in Naples, as she charged me, and doubtless others, a toll of one lire to cross her well defended territory!

On New Year's Eve I was invited to a party in the centre of Naples and introduced to some friends of the Borrelli family who lived nearby: Donna Amanda and her family had recently bought a television set. Friends were subsequently often invited to their home to watch special programmes. As television was still very much a new form of home entertainment we were glad to share in it – especially in a family home.

From time to time, Tonino (Ciccio Paolo's brother-in-law) came to Naples from Cassano, and one evening introduced me to the Trocadero nightclub. The Trocadero was a top class club situated on the sea front in the Santa Lucia district. It attracted the Naples glitterati with its lively bands and dancing. I got to know the musicians in the club and when the leader and singer became ill, I was asked to take his place by singing for a few weeks. It was a tremendous opportunity and gave me just the kind of experience I needed to build my confidence. It was also great fun!

My singing lessons continued and as Maestro Giannini, my singing teacher, was also a conductor he asked me to join his band on tour the following summer. I was thrilled. Although I wouldn't be paid to perform, I recognised that it was another opportunity to gain experience alongside established artists. The band, including several well known singers, was booked to perform at a festa held in the city of Potenza in the South.

We travelled from Naples to Potenza by coach, enabling me to see the breath-taking Amalfi coast for the first time. I soaked up the atmosphere and listened closely to the other singers, determined to learn all I could from their performances. When at last it was my turn, I sang the popular "Cancello tra le Rose", giving it my best shot and feeling every inch the professional. At the end of my performance a large crowd gathered eager to talk to me and waving their autograph books under my nose. It was a brief and glorious taste of stardom!

In the spring of 1957 my brother Franco, who had been in the army in Como, was demobbed and returned to Cassano. Franco had previously been a farm worker, but had no intention of returning to work the land. Like me, he was keen to become a professional musician. He had been given the opportunity to play the saxophone both in the army band and in a swing band which played the Glenn Miller repertoire and these experiences had only increased his enthusiasm. He asked if he could join me in Naples to try to find work as a musician. Consequently, Franco stayed with me on and off for several months, and as he had no money I was required to pay for his food and lodging. I was keen to help – he was my brother after all – but at the beginning of July I found that I was six weeks in arrears with the rent, a debt which put me under enormous pressure. I knew that Mario Giovannini wanted me to go back to work at Bar Clipper, so I decided to return to Rimini, where I would earn more money, to work to pay my debts. In order to travel from Naples to Rimini I plucked up courage and asked my friend Donna Amanda if I could borrow the fare of 4000 lire, which I promised to pay back as soon as possible. She kindly agreed, understanding both my anxiety and my need to put things right.

I left Naples and turned up at the Bar Clipper unannounced, to the delight of Mario Giovannini and his wife. They welcomed me warmly, sat me down to eat and as I told them my story I mentioned the debt I owed to Donna Amanda: a debt of both kindness

and cash. Mario Giovaninni generously offered to pay the money back, knowing that I would soon be able to repay him by working. I was overwhelmed at his generosity and faith in me and sent the money to Donna Amanda immediately. I also explained my working arrangements to Sig.ra Borrelli, my landlady in Naples, so that she would be assured that my overdue rent would also soon be paid.

Franco, meanwhile, stayed in Naples and found a job looking after the stores in the Bar Cristallo. As he only worked during the day he was able to pursue his ambition to become a professional musician by playing in various bands in the evenings. He gradually became well known in Naples: his success meaning that my brotherly debts had been worth the burden.

In between my work and my singing lessons there may not have been much time for romance – but there was enough.

Whilst I was still working in the bar in Rimini I began to receive anonymous telephone calls from a girl. Eventually I discovered, through a friend, that the girl's name was Ivana. Her family owned several souvenir shops in Rimini and she was keen to get to know me. We met occasionally when I was free and began to grow quite close. She went on to write to me for some time – something which made a huge difference when I was later away on National Service. Ivana was not to be the love of my life however: but the girl destined for that particular role was closer than I realised.

I met a large number of English and Scandinavian tourists in the bar and was particularly intrigued by the English visitors, wanting to know what sort of lives they lived. In an effort to find out in the most pleasant way, I befriended two English girls, Barbara and Jean, who often came into the bar together. We had very limited language in common, but enjoyed one another's company regardless, communicating with sign language and lively behaviour.

Barbara, particularly, had something about her. She would wear striking and stylish dresses bought at Dickens and Jones department store in London, where she worked. One was green and spotted with bows at the shoulders; another was a particularly elegant navy blue with a wide white collar. She was lively and determined and not at all like other girls who I had met before. She seemed to know her own mind – and she was great fun.

Barbara and Jean, to my delight, seemed to take more of an interest in me than the other girls did and one day asked if I would have my photograph taken with them. I was more than happy to be pictured with two lovely young English women.

So we all posed together and I looked forward to the results which they promised to send me once they had returned to England.

One evening, Barbara came into the bar alone to have a cup of cappuccino and to listen to me singing. Unknown to me, it was almost the end of her holiday. We still couldn't say very much to each other: I was busy in the bar or singing and my English was limited to little more than 'Good Evening' and 'Hello' – but we must have communicated somehow!

Towards the end of the evening Barbara was offered a glass of sparkling wine by an English gentleman and by about one o'clock in the morning I noticed that she looked a bit tipsy. I didn't quite trust the Englishman – or any Englishman for that matter – to look after her. So in my poor and broken English I suggested to Barbara that I might accompany her to her

Rimini, Sep 1957 outside Clipper Bar. Mario & Barbara first encounter

hotel. To my delight, she agreed. I knew that any attempt at English conversation would be over almost before it began and certainly wouldn't last until we reached our destination. So I sang to her as we walked along the dark, empty streets – she simply smiled and looked at me with her searching eyes. When we reached the door of her hotel I decided to be bold. There, in the romantic moonlight, I said goodbye and kissed her goodnight. I walked home filled with bravado and elation, not knowing that a song and a kiss had really started something.

The following day I wasn't at work in the bar: I had travelled to another singing competition in Castrocaro Terme. When I returned I was teased and told with some amusement that the *Inglesina* had come to say goodbye to me before returning to England. It was Barbara, and she had been upset to miss me. Hearing this news I suddenly wished she could know that I missed her too.

A few days later an unusual letter arrived at the bar – with an English postmark – and it was addressed to me. It contained the promised photograph of Barbara, Jean and me in my white jacket and bow tie. Folded around it was a note containing something very precious and infinitely promising: Barbara's address in London.

She obviously wanted me to stay in touch. I was elated and looked again at the photograph. I didn't know it at the time, but the lovely girl in the spotted dress smiling up at me from that photograph, was my wife to be. We had embarked on a holiday romance that would last a lifetime.

CHAPTER FOUR:

Il Sospiro (The Sigh)

The night I asked you to be mine,
You looked at me and with a sigh...

In the autumn of that year I received a note from my Aunt – *Zia* -Caterina in America. She explained that her youngest son, Geno, was about to arrive in Naples by boat. Franco and I knew that Geno had recently graduated from Harvard University because a graduation photograph had been sent to my grandmother. It showed Geno in mortar board and gown, convincing her that he was a judge. Our family was in awe of Geno because of his academic achievements, so it was with a degree of nervousness as well as excitement that I prepared to be the first of our branch of the family to welcome him to Italy.

I knew I would recognise Geno as I had seen his photograph. I tried to imagine him without the mortar board and gown, but assumed that with all his success he would be rather full of himself. I could not have been more wrong.

I spotted Geno from some distance. He was dressed very smartly (for an American!) in black trousers and a check jacket with two side vents. Looking for something to criticise in this supposedly smug American, I noticed that the vents were very short – about 6". The Italian fashion was to have vents of up to 10". When I later commented on this fashion fact Geno exclaimed, "What?! This is the latest fashion in the States!"

I quickly explained to Geno, that although Franco was now well established as a musician, the accommodation we shared was very basic: the only alternative for Geno was a hotel room. Geno explained that as a student he had been used to the less than luxurious, and was keen to stay with us. He quickly made himself at home, joined in willingly with all our activities and proved himself to be far from the smug American cousin we had anticipated. It was the beginning of a close and long-lasting friendship.

Geno remained with us for a few days before going first to Florence to study Italian and later to the International University of Perugia. Whenever he could he returned to Naples to see us or to visit our relatives in the South.

On one of these visits I asked him if he would write a letter to Barbara in English. We had been writing to each other since the arrival of the photograph, but I had no choice but to write in Italian. Consequently, Barbara always needed to ask an Italian member of the staff at Dickens and Jones in London, where she worked, to translate my words. Not the clearest or most straightforward way to correspond or the ideal way in which to share love and affection in private! Geno was delighted to help, and although he could have written a list of animals, birds, vegetables and fruit for all I know, I had to trust that for once Barbara could read my words in her own language.

In March 1958 Geno visited us in Naples once more for an entirely different reason: to see me off at the beginning of my National Service.

I spent the first three months at Casale Monferrato in Northern Italy, at a training centre, before being sent to the regimental barracks in Genova.

As I struggled to adjust to home-sickness and army discipline, an event occurred which was to change my army life for the better. The army band master began recruiting, looking particularly for anyone who was able to play the side drums. Luckily, I qualified, just for being able to play a drum roll, and was accepted as one of two drummers immediately. My drumming partner, however, proved to be both left-handed and heavy-handed, repeatedly breaking the drumsticks. He would also pick up a beat out of time. Because I couldn't read music, it was assumed that the missed beat was down to me. Quietly indignant, I politely suggested to the bandmaster that I step out of the band while they played with just my drumming partner. When the beat was missed once again it was established without doubt that my heavy handed colleague was to blame and I was exonerated.

We were transferred to Como barracks for a week-long special event where we were housed in a large dormitory – an explosive mix of experienced soldiers and new recruits. One night, the dark, sticky air of the dormitory reverberated with the deep, throaty, snores of a young recruit. No end of firm but pointed whispering leading to a well timed yell stopped the row, so one of the older men crept across the dormitory floor and flung a jug of water into the sleeping face of the younger man in a final attempt to shut him up. Suddenly there was uproar as the young soldier began waving his arms around as if he was swimming, much to the amusement of his audience. Once he was fully awake, he began to climb down from his bunk dripping and furious to angrily kick the now empty jug out of the way and to take his revenge. Instead, he caught his foot on the corner of the metal bed frame and fell, breaking his leg and howling out in agony. The lights were switched on and he was rushed to the infirmary. No one dared to reveal the background to the accident – or the perpetrator. On the nights following, I made sure I kept a heavy boot handy in case anyone approached me with a wet wake-up call.

During marching rehearsals, we played one particular march which we all enjoyed. The Sicilian who played the brass bass had a wicked and daring sense of humour and would repeat the same musical

Genova Barracks Dec. 1958.
Mario & friends privileged soldiers in civilian clothes

Casale Monferrato Training Centre, May 1958

phrase as a joke. It meant that the rest of the band always had to follow him before playing the rest of the tune. This must have irritated the band master no end, but there was little he could do about it.

On our return to Casale we continued with our training, learning how to handle guns and how to shoot, march and salute while carrying a gun: all routine necessities for the modern Italian soldier – the skills of a finely honed fighting force! Yet every time we marched, there would always be one soldier who found it impossible to pace in time, often with hilarious results.

On the serious side, marching reflected the order and discipline we were required to demonstrate and when a platoon of soldiers went out for the evening on leave, I was often chosen to lead them out of the barracks in an orderly fashion. Once we were dismissed, however, the 'orderly' behaviour pretty much went with us! On our evenings off, we sat outside the bars, chatting and laughing, soon discovering that the town contained more mosquitoes than men, surrounded as it was by rice fields and water. So great was the problem that the bar owner would spray our legs with DT. Unlike the mosquitoes, the girls ignored us, presumably because their parents had warned them about getting involved with soldiers. To show our annoyance we would throw our hats on the ground in disgust, ignoring the likelihood of court-martial if we were found out.

Later that summer we were transferred to our respective regiments: in my case to the 157th regiment in Genova.

When I arrived in Genova, the band master of the regiment was waiting for me and I was soon practising with the band almost every day. This assignment saved me many dreary hours of routine duties, although I did enjoy one routine job as a spoilsport. I became part of a patrol whose job it was to pick up all those soldiers who were stretching their evening passes by staying out in the town too late.

In the middle of the summer the regiment were moved to the hills for six weeks for exercises. More than anything else it gave us an opportunity to escape the heat and mosquitoes, if not, the girls.

As a band we were asked to entertain not only the soldiers but the people from the neighbouring village and a special dance was held in the square. It began sedately enough with everyone arriving nervously and politely greeting one another, but once the band began to play defences were dropped, dancing began and villagers and soldiers alike joined in together in party spirit. The major in charge of the battalion danced with the local ladies and at the end of the evening gave me a generous tip.

One of my regimental duties involved carrying a 40 lbs radio transmitter – used to communicate with other battalions – to wherever it was needed. One morning as I drove with the transmitter to the chosen site, I happened to tell the 2nd Lieutenant in charge of transmission, who was sitting alongside me, that I was a trained telephone operator. He immediately ordered the driver of the vehicle to turn round, as he needed a telephone operator back at headquarters. That chance conversation meant that I remained a telephone operator for the rest of my army service.

Genova Summer 1958. Mario and two soldier friends

Our summer exercises completed, we returned to the barracks at Genova where I was assigned to the main switchboard. My telephone duties meant that I had special privileges: I didn't have to sleep in the dormitory – risking a watery attack – but slept in a bunk bed near the switchboard. Neither did I have to queue for my meals, as the telephone needed to be available for use at all times. My privileged position also meant that I gradually got to know the officers, from the Colonel-in-Chief to the Marshals, as well as their interesting habits.

The Colonel, second in charge of the regiment, would ring me at exactly three o'clock every afternoon to ask me to call a certain number. A sexy female voice would answer, which I soon discovered belonged to his girlfriend. On some occasions I would cheekily attempt to listen to their conversation.

Some time later I was asked by a regimental captain to form a similar romantic connection by telephone. As he was the captain in charge of food and beverages, I was consequently rewarded for my intrigue and discretion with anything I needed from the stores – including wine, fruit and cakes.

I was still writing regularly to Barbara – although still mostly in 'to be translated' or 'has been translated' Italian – and was delighted to learn that she was planning to return to Italy to take up a post as an au pair in Turin. When I asked in a letter if she couldn't manage to come to Genova, she replied that I shouldn't complain – Turin was a lot nearer to Genova than London!

Even as our relationship became more serious, our letters still needed a 'go between' and I increasingly recognised the need to learn Barbara's

Rimini Riccione Aug. 1958 on holiday from army

language. However, one particular effort to improve my English inadvertently landed me in hot water.

A group of officers were travelling by train when they met an attractive young lady: Aglaia Romagnolo. When they discovered that she was a music magazine columnist and told her about my desire to sing, she suggested that I should get in touch with her. In the course of our subsequent conversation, I mentioned to her that Barbara was coming from England and Aglaia told me that she both spoke and taught English. So we arranged for her to give me some English lessons. I was so pleased about meeting Aglaia that I telephoned the home of the officer responsible to tell him about the meeting and to thank him. The officer's wife answered and I innocently chatted away, telling her all about her husband's contact and how helpful Aglaia had been to me. A few days later the officer came to see me. He was irate and asked if I knew what I had done: I didn't. His wife – perhaps a little more suspicious and jealous than most – had thought that he was having an affair with 'this Aglaia' and the only way to clear things up was for me to meet his wife outside the barracks to put things straight. Otherwise, he said, he would have me transferred to another regiment. The meeting with the officer's wife was duly arranged. I told her that she had no need to worry as Aglaia could not possibly compete with her elegance and good looks. I explained that even my connection with Aqlaia was one of a purely artistic nature. I must have been convincing, because she believed me – and I stayed with the regiment.

As the date of Barbara's arrival in Italy approached, I began to realise the magnitude of what she had done. She had been working as an accounts supervisor at Dickens and Jones in Regent Street and had given up her job to spend time in Italy in order to get to know me better. I was overjoyed that this lovely English girl was prepared to go to such lengths to see me again. Her liveliness so appealed to me: the way she stamped her foot to make a point; even her slightly twisted front tooth was somehow attractive. She also had such a penetrating way of looking at me, as if she was studying the very depths of my soul: I didn't think I would ever be able to hide very much from this young woman! Coming from a different culture meant that she intrigued me and I was longing to know more and more about her.

England, 1940. Barbara Aged 5, Mother, Baby Leslie, Father & Sister Helen

Barbara was due to visit me in Genova, en route to Turin, just before Christmas, so as I had some leave owing, we arranged to meet in Genova, visit Aglaia briefly and then spend my leave at my parents' home in Cassano.

When Barbara arrived, there was nothing but

delight between us at the sight of each other. We went straight to Aglaia's home for lunch, where we soon discovered that Aglaia's spoken English was not quite up to scratch: Barbara had difficulty understanding her! The only way we could communicate was by writing our questions and answers down on paper and passing them to Aglaia to translate from the written word.

The following day, as we explored the town together, we tried to use a pocket dictionary in an attempt to make conversation. But we soon abandoned the dictionary in favour

Cassano, January 1959. Barbara & Peppino looking at a dictionary and Enzo serenading

of Pidgin English and Italian, with gestures. Despite the language barrier, something about Barbara made me realise that this girl was in need of love and affection.

We travelled to Acquaviva – en route to Cassano – arriving early in the morning, and I took Barbara into the bar where I had previously worked for the Gentile family. At that time in the morning it was full of men in noisy and animated conversation, drinking their coffee before going to work. As we walked in, the conversation stopped at the sight of a pretty English girl, eliciting murmurs of "*che bella stac*": 'what a beautiful mare'.

After Barbara and I had enjoyed coffee and pastries, my former boss Sr.Gentile took me to one side and said that he had a serious matter to discuss with me and would I please return to see him as soon as possible. Puzzled, we went on our way to Cassano, three miles away and when I called into the bar a couple of days later he asked me to accompany him to his home nearby. There, he unbuckled his leather belt in readiness and accused me of having sex with his daughter Maria, some time before. He said that Maria had shared this intimate information with her sister, Francesca, and in his eyes this meant that I had to marry Maria. I admitted that I had been in love with Maria years before when I had worked in the bar, but I strongly denied having sex with her. It was obvious from the flashing of his eyes and the flexing of his belt that he didn't believe me. Eventually, I managed to calm him down by promising that I would think seriously about the matter and return to discuss it at a later date. In fact I never went back. It was not the kind of confrontation I needed with Barbara in tow!

Barbara responded well to the warm welcome my family gave her in Cassano - despite the fact that both were unfamiliar with the culture of the other.

Our first family meal together began with a large plate of spaghetti topped with a small amount of sauce. Barbara was overwhelmed by the amount of pasta but

Cassano January 1959. *FROM LEFT*: *Mother Alessandra, Maria, Giuseppe, Rosa, Mario & Father Antonio, Barbara, Saverio & little niece Isabella celebrating!*

politely struggled to eat it all. She refused the second helping offered by my mother, who had also assumed that all English people drank copious amounts of alcohol with their meals and had given Barbara a glass of neat gin!

The language difficulties and the domestic arrangements were certainly a challenge, as were the differences in personal habits. Barbara pointed out that our very Italian family habit of eating with our mouths open so as to chat at the same time was hard for her to cope with and would be considered very coarse in England. So I gently told my parents and from then on we all tried to keep our mouths firmly shut, even if only when eating.

Over the following days, Barbara and I walked through Cassano meeting friends and relatives, all of whom were curious to meet this young lady from England. Most greeted her warmly and extravagantly with a kiss on both cheeks prompting Barbara to ask me exactly how many relatives I had!

But not everyone was warm and welcoming: when we bumped into my aunt Isabella, my father's sister, I happily explained that Barbara was my girlfriend, expecting the same warm reception. But she gave Barbara a disapproving look saying that she hoped I would not think of marrying this girl as she was a foreigner. I also heard girls from the village openly debating what I found especially attractive about this English girl. But I had met so many lovely English and Scandinavian girls while in Rimini, I had already decided that I was not going to marry an Italian!

At that time it was still traditional for the eldest child to be married before the others. It was my duty therefore to step aside to let my older brother Peppino (short for Giuseppe) get to know Barbara. When I explained this to Barbara she was shocked and said that I was her boyfriend and she was definitely not willing to transfer her affections to my brother, however much she enjoyed his company.

Barbara found the difference in cultural more fascinating, especially the way the men of the village congregated in the square in the evenings to chat. She struggled with the custom which dictated that women did not go into bars or cinemas and insisted on going to both with her head held high.

Her English tea-drinking habits were also challenging. When she asked for tea in one bar, an ancient camomile tea maker appeared from the depths of a cupboard. It was covered in cobwebs such was the rarity of her request.

After spending a wonderful time in Cassano, we returned to Genova. I took up my military duties once more and Barbara travelled on to Turin to begin her new job. During the following weeks she wrote to me as often as she could, telling me about her new life as an au pair.

The Turin family consisted of a grandfather – a senior member of the judiciary – and a grandmother; their daughter who was separated from her husband and her six year old son, Massimo. They lived in a mansion just outside Turin with extensive manicured grounds and an enormous hall dominated by a great curving staircase. They kept a chauffeur and two resident servants who lived on the ground floor and all the members of the family had their own private suite of rooms.

Barbara soon discovered that Massimo was very spoilt and that she was expected to do everything for him, including playing on the floor with Massimo *and* his Alsatian dog. The family were demanding and unreasonable and she quickly realised that her position was impossible. So she handed in her notice.

She wrote to me explaining that she intended to join me in Genova. I understood her situation and knew she could do little else. But as I was a soldier, her predicament put me in a very difficult situation, added to which I had to try to find a solution to her accommodation problems.

I spoke to Marshal Bartolozzi, who was in charge of the barracks printing works, to see if he might be able to help. He assured me that his wife would be pleased to have Barbara to stay, as their daughter wished to learn English.

So Barbara arrived in Genova and stayed with the family for the next few weeks while she looked for another job. It wasn't always an easy arrangement: Sig.ra Bartolozzi insisted on bathing Barbara because it reminded her of former days when she had been a personal maid to an important Libyan lady!

When I rang to speak to Barbara the signora would answer the telephone and engage me in a long conversation, after which she would ring off, completely forgetting that Barbara was the one I wanted to speak to! Meanwhile Barbara would have to wait until I rang again.

In the evenings the Marshal and his wife would go to the Officers' Mess taking Barbara with them. On one of these occasions, the Marshal told Barbara to use the telephone in the Mess to speak to me. This telephone was for the sole use of the duty officer, so when the phone rang I answered "Yes Sir" and was astonished to hear Barbara saying "Ciao Mario, this is me, Barbara", to the amusement of the Marshal.

Soon afterwards, Barbara confided that the Marshal was becoming altogether too familiar in his behaviour towards her, making the securing of some alternative accommodation an urgent need. So we found her lodgings with a Neapolitan family who lived near the barracks.

Our communication – Pidgin and otherwise – gradually became easier and in my time off we took long walks during which the subject of marriage was inevitably raised. Barbara told me that she was willing to take a course of study to become a Roman Catholic, but that thinking ahead she had reservations about some Italian customs, especially regarding priorities in childbirth. She had heard that custom dictated that if there were life threatening problems during the birth of a baby, the survival of the baby was paramount. Barbara made me promise that if this happened I would insist that she should survive instead of the baby. However Barbara might feel later, I agreed wholeheartedly. We couldn't have known then that Barbara would go on to defiantly – even miraculously – survive much worse than difficult childbirth.

In February 1959 Barbara moved to the home of Dr Savoretti and his family, again as an au pair. Dr Savoretti was a leading obstetrician in Genova and lived with his family in a very large and glamorous apartment in the centre of the town, making it much easier for me to meet Barbara during her time off.

My wages were 1100 lire every ten days, but by the time I had taken Barbara out, bought her a cappuccino and chocolate – *Bacio Perugina* – and paid our bus fares, half of my wages had disappeared. The buses were frequently full and as the ticket collector sat in the centre of the bus it was impossible to reach him so we often got off the bus without paying our fare. Barbara thought this was dishonest, but I pointed out that with the money I'd saved I could buy her another *Bacio*!

Barbara's appointment with the Savoretti family the children used did not fulfil its promise. Sometimes she would ask me the meaning of words she had heard and to my surprise they were swear words. The family did not keep to the terms of their contract with Barbara and would change her day off at a moment's notice or delay paying her wages. Sig.ra Savoretti eventually asked to speak to me and complained about Barbara's behaviour. I listened to what she had to say and then quietly told her that Barbara would be leaving within the next few days. As far as I was concerned Barbara's behaviour was not in question: she had discovered that the Grandmother had stolen her brooch and some of her clothes and had an unpleasant habit of peeping through keyholes to spy on her.

Just as Barbara was in the process of leaving the Savoretti family my brother Franco arrived in Genova with his band. Barbara moved into a hotel room with the girlfriend of a band member, which gave her the space and time she needed to look for another job and find new accommodation. She quickly found lodgings near the barracks with a Sig.ra Cordano, and secured a job teaching English at the Berlitz School of Languages, while also giving private lessons to people in their homes.

I would meet Barbara at lunch time after school, when she would often have made out a shopping list for the local grocer's shop. In Italy in those days it was unusual for anyone to make out a shopping list unless they were a maid. Consequently, the grocer would often ignore Barbara and serve everyone else in the queue first; probably assuming that she could not be a respectable girl because of her attachment to a soldier. Barbara's landlady refused to allow her to wash some of my clothes for the same reason. But Barbara endeared herself to people, and once the grocer found out that she was an English teacher and that it was normal for an English person to make out a shopping list he became more friendly. Barbara's relationship with Sig.ra Cordano, her landlady, also improved as she gradually gained her affection. Sig.ra Cordano and her family had many a laugh at Barbara's attempts at spoken Italian. She would call the landlady's son-in-law 'callo' (meaning a corn) instead of pronouncing Carlo with an 'r' and referred to knees as *finocchi* meaning fennel instead of *ginocchi*.

We settled down to our adjacent working lives and made the most of seeing as much of each other as we could.

One of my proudest moments occurred one commemorative day in April when I was asked to beat out the drum in front of the regiment: we marched through the town to the applause and cheers of the crowd and the fluttering of occasional handkerchiefs.

On another occasion there was a special parade within the barracks, to which I was able to invite Barbara and Sig.ra Cordano as guests. The band played while

Miramare-Rimini. August 1959. Mario recently demobbed from the National Service with Barbara

the rest of the regiment marched, the sunshine bouncing off the brass of the instruments. I even twiddled the drumsticks as an acknowledgement to the special presence of Barbara and Sig.ra Cordano.

Soon afterwards I became ill with an infection and was ordered to stay in the barracks infirmary. Barbara came to visit me bringing a basket of goodies: bread rolls, fruit and hot chocolate. At the entrance to the barracks the soldiers on duty surrounded this pretty girl and asked her what she wanted. She pretended not to know much Italian, but using a few crocodile tears and feminine wiles managed to convey that I was in the infirmary and that she wanted desperately to see me. The duty officer softened and relented and asked one of the guards to accompany her to my bedside. The guard duly marched into the ward ahead of her and, as was correct behaviour, stood to attention in the middle of the room. As Barbara followed him in, all the sick soldiers miraculously recovered, sat upright and began combing their hair, while I was staggered at her resourcefulness and the power she so obviously exerted – as guard of honour, indeed! Surprised and delighted, I talked to Barbara about her experience on the way in for some time, until I suddenly realised that the poor guard was still standing to attention in the centre of the room. I ordered him to stand at ease until the time came for him to escort Barbara out again.

Barbara's work permit was due to expire the following June, but as she wanted to continue to work in Italy she was advised to go to Nice to stay overnight on the understanding that on the return journey her permit would be extended for another six months. Her contract with the Berlitz School ended at the same time so she began looking for other employment, added to which I was due to go to the Piedmont Mountains with the regiment until August, prior to being demobbed. In an attempt to help Barbara find another job I wrote to Sig.Giovannini in Rimini to see whether he could employ Barbara for the summer season. He agreed that Barbara could work in the bar and stay at their home and that she would be paid 15,000 lire a month. It was a kind and generous offer which we accepted. I was able to go away content in the knowledge that Barbara would be staying with people I knew who would take good care of her.

Barbara had an interesting stay with the family as Sig. Giovannini; his wife, Nanda; his son, Marcello and his grandmother all lived together. Barbara found that Marcello was spoilt, even at 14 his mother referred to him as 'the baby'. Barbara told me that although the younger members of the family did their best to welcome her, the old lady was never able to do so and accused her of killing her son in the war, simply because she was English. Neither would the family allow Barbara to have a

Rimini Miramare Summer 1959. FROM LEFT: *Two Customers then Mario Giovannini, Mario, Barbara an d the gentleman from The Savoy Group and his wife*

bath or do her washing because of a water shortage, necessitating a trip to the public baths in the square and a special effort to make her clothes last longer than usual before washing them.

As my army service came to an end, demob day was full of emotional farewells. Not only had I done my duty for my country but I had known some hilarious times, made some good friendships and achieved a sense of accomplishment.

I returned to Rimini where I was met by Barbara, having arranged to work in the bar with her for the rest of the season. I slept on a camp bed in the basement, next to the firewood, but at least Barbara would come down early in the morning – fully dressed I hasten to add – to wake me up.

When we wanted an espresso coffee to finish our lunch we always offered to pay for it but Sig. Giovannini wouldn't hear of it, saying that we must not pay because we worked for him. Yet instead of providing two small cups of espresso coffee he would give us one – to share. It was clear that the business was not doing well, and it wasn't long before Barbara's pay was reduced to the equivalent of a pound a week.

But we were at least able to be together, and when we had a rare hour off we would go to the beach to relax. Unable to resist the opportunity for a light-hearted dig at the Italians, Barbara would remark on the litter, collecting and binning it whilst berating us for our untidiness: I would point out that she could not educate a whole nation single handed. Barbara agreed that she couldn't – but that she could start with me.

The fact that Barbara was English inevitably attracted English customers into the bar where she could engage in some welcome English conversation, with me adding my Pidgin English comments whenever possible. We became so friendly with one couple, Maureen and Arthur Disney, that Arthur would later agree to be the Best Man at our wedding.

One smart couple who often came to the bar were particularly important as far as the next stage of our lives was concerned, as we soon discovered that he was a representative of the Savoy group of hotels. In conversation with Barbara he promised to look for work for me in England. Barbara would soon be returning home and it was soon to be my turn to cross Europe in order to get to know *her* better.

CHAPTER FIVE:
An Italian in England

In September 1959 Barbara returned home leaving me with a feeling of emptiness and sadness. But I focused on looking forward to seeing her again. I had already applied for my work permit to enable me to join her in England. Now both of us had to learn to wait patiently.

At the beginning of October Barbara received some good news from the Forte company in Regent Street. She told me that they had acquired a work permit for me to take up a position as a commis waiter and that she was forwarding the papers to me. I immediately applied for a passport while trying to obtain references from my previous employers – wisely excluding the Gentile family.

My passport did not arrive. I discovered that it had been delayed because the Arch Priest of Cassano had told the authorities in Bari that I did not attend church regularly – an important element of my application. So I went to see my old acquaintance Sig. Cafaro in Acquaviva, whose brother was also an Archbishop, and explained my position. He promised to see what he could do.

Barbara wrote every two or three days, becoming increasingly desperate. The contents of her letters may have been largely serious and full of 'when?' and 'If only' but I often lay in bed shaking with laughter at her eccentric spelling and the way she expressed herself in Italian. My mother used to ask me what on earth Barbara had written that made me laugh so much.

Finally, at the beginning of December, Sig. Cafaro's efforts at intervention paid off and my passport arrived at last. With great excitement I went to purchase my rail ticket to Victoria.

I was at last ready to leave Italy for England – and for Barbara.

My departure date was fixed for 12th December 1959, and as preparations gathered apace, everybody in Cassano became aware that I was leaving Italy for a foreign country. Most had advice to impart and anxieties to share. My grandmother was first in the queue: "Mario" she said "I am worried for you. How you are going to manage in England without wine, with missing the southern Italian cooking?" "Don't worry Nonna." I replied, "They drink lots of beer there."

I was also told by numerous Italians who had read about London that dull boiled potatoes were a main part of the English diet; that it was bitterly cold all the time and that there was thick smog creeping from every corner of the British Isles. I found it hard to believe that the sun never shone on the English. But my mother made sure that I would be well protected with warm clothes. She gave me a thick woollen vest, a pair of less than enchanting Long Johns, a very warm suit, a heavy coat and a snug woolly hat. She also provided me with a good supply of olive oil and a cooked stuffed rabbit.

I finally set off to fond farewells and winsome worrying with £6 in my pocket on a train journey that would take 24 hours. I knew the English put milk in their tea, but that wasn't the Italian way, so I when I changed trains at Milan Central Station, I bought a kilo of lemons to take with me for my tea – just in case.

I arrived at Victoria Station on a cold December day which gave me every indication that the fears of my relatives had been entirely based on truth. I was also expecting, as was the Italian way, that all of Barbara's family would be there to meet me. But Barbara was by herself: a solitary figure with a wide smile. Suddenly the temperature rose.

Barbara stared in disbelief at my plentiful personal supply of olive oil and chuckled at my layers of warm clothes: the stuffed rabbit I kept under wraps like a closet magician.

We travelled to South Croydon by train and then caught a bus to Warlingham, finally walking the short distance to Barbara's home, where I was greeted by her mother, Helena. Barbara's brother Leslie was sitting in the lounge in an armchair reading a newspaper, so Barbara introduced me to him saying, "Leslie, this is Mario." Leslie lowered his paper briefly, said "Hello' and went back to his reading. As an Italian used to warm welcomes and extravagant hospitality I was shocked by this very casual greeting and by the fact that both Barbara's younger brother John and sister Helen were out at the time of my arrival. I wondered what my mother's response would be to such behaviour.

I was asked if I would like a cup of tea which Barbara brought to me: it was made with milk. I told her that I had brought some fresh lemons from Italy for my tea, but Barbara replied, "You're in England now and from now on you drink tea with milk." To this day I do not know what happened to the lemons or the olive oil...and as for the rabbit...

As my job in the theatre restaurant of the *Talk of the Town* in London did not start for a week or so, Barbara took the opportunity to show me around the area and introduce me to the capital.

We went into London to find some accommodation for me as close to work as possible, and called in at Forte's head office in Regent Street so that I could introduce myself and meet Marion, the secretary, who had been such a help to us in arranging my work.

Now it was Barbara who was at ease and I who felt very much a foreigner.

So much about England seemed either unfamiliar, or as if it had been briefly glimpsed through films, magazines or hearsay. The English way was often puzzling, sometimes embarrassing and often, to me at least, ridiculous. Suddenly, it was me who was struggling to learn a new language and Barbara who had the last laugh. She would get her revenge when we were travelling by bus, mischievously asking me to repeat phrases: "Two three penny tickets to the Swan and Sugarloaf" or "Two three penny tickets to Hyde Park Corner", giggling at the mixed up linguistic commotion that resulted.

I found accommodation in Kensington, sharing a room with another Mario who also worked at *The Talk of the Town*. He came from Rome, had lived in London for some time and drove a sports car. This proved very convenient for me as he gave me a lift home in the early hours of the morning when we finished work.

Whilst some elements of English life were bewildering, I found the bright Christmas lights of London exciting, especially the window displays in Oxford and Regent Street that I had heard so much about in Italy. I would walk through the streets, dodging the Christmas shoppers and absorbing all that made London unique, pinching myself, still amazed that I was actually there.

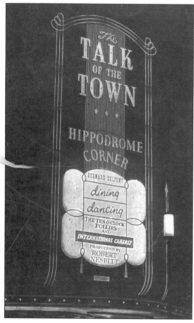

The highlight of my time at the *Talk of the Town* was that very first New Year's Eve. There was a full house, a star-studded bill, a lively well-dressed crowd and a floor show which was shown on national television. I had to juggle the trays of food past the television cameras as they spun to and fro to capture the best shots.

The restaurant was full of the stars we would now call 'celebrities': Joan Collins and her husband Anthony Newley; Leslie Phillips and the American actor, Van Johnson; the Forte family and Bernard Delfont who jointly owned the theatre restaurant.

I was amazed to see how the English celebrated New Year's Eve. When Big Ben struck midnight chaos broke out, balloons popped and everybody started kissing everyone else, before breaking into a chorus of Auld Lang Syne. The festivities went on until two-thirty in the morning when the restaurant finally emptied, the debris was cleared and 'the other Mario' and I returned home in his car, exhausted from work but buoyed up by the celebrations.

After a few weeks I managed to find a room to rent in Romilly Street, Soho, with a Neapolitan family. It was within walking distance of the *Talk of the Town* and, as much as I enjoyed Mario's company and his sports car, it gave me my independence. I had no idea of the reputation of Soho – although I was warned about it by my colleagues and by Barbara who found my naivety about my new living location almost as hilarious as my Long Johns.

Every Sunday I went by bus to Barbara's home in Warlingham, where I gradually got to know her family.

Barbara's youngest brother, John, wanted to test me out, so he took me to the local pub and plied me gin and tonics until he reached number six. To his astonishment I remained upright, whilst he had begun to slide under the table at number three and had stopped, hardly able to open his mouth, let alone drink, by number four.

Helen, Barbara's sister, was by contrast, gentle and polite but we couldn't really make conversation and Barbara had to act as interpreter.

I was glad of my woolly jumpers, however much hilarity they had caused: the only heating in Barbara's freezing house was a coal fire. One Sunday, as the family were lighting it, the chimney caught fire necessitating a call for the fire brigade. Because the fire had been caused by an unswept chimney the family were charged £5 – paid by Barbara's mother's boyfriend, who often spent Sunday with us.

Leslie, the eldest in the family, was a Jehovah's Witness (which I had never heard of) and a postman. He began talking to me about the Jehovah's Witnesses and asked me to read their magazines. When I told him that I couldn't read English he explained that this wasn't a problem as he could get some written in Italian, which he duly did. I cast my eye over them briefly and then posted them to my mother, knowing that she enjoyed reading. Never in my wildest dreams did it occur to me that one day she would become a Jehovah's Witness as a result of an English postman in Surrey.

I gradually became accustomed to the English way of doing things – unless they involved anything Italian!

Barbara and I took a day trip to Brighton where we noticed a cafe blackboard advertising Spaghetti Bolognese: a rare sight in 1960. Intrigued, we went inside and ordered it in some excited anticipation. When it arrived I was horrified to see that a tin of Spaghetti Bolognese had been heated up, cut in half vertically and served up on a plate in a solid block. I couldn't even begin to think about eating it, so I sent it back. I was offered an omelette as an alternative but even this arrived swimming in some sort of oil – probably engine. Because I was so hungry I managed to eat it. When we somewhat reluctantly paid the bill the cafe owner remarked that a member of his staff had eaten the pasta and had declared it "very nice". I told him that it may have been "very nice" to his member of staff but it certainly wasn't to an Italian!

Barbara took a job with the First National City Bank of New York in Lombard Street at a salary of £16 per week and I enrolled at a college in Rupert Street, Soho, for three mornings a week, to learn basic English. I found a second job working as a lunch-hour extra in an Italian Restaurant, also in Soho, until I was asked by the management of the Cafe Royal to work the lunchtime shift in their restaurant where I also worked occasional evenings. The incentive for all this hard work was our future – and my promise to send money back to Italy to help my family.

Barbara and I would meet at about five o'clock every afternoon when she left the bank and before I went to my job at *The Talk of the Town*. The more time we spent together the more we wanted to stay together – forever.

Ever practical, Barbara explained the benefits of marrying before the end of the tax year. She also pointed out that it might be a good idea to marry sooner rather than later while she was young enough to have children – after all, she was almost

26! Eventually, during a telephone conversation I proposed that we should get married the following March to Barbara's great delight.

Plans were to be made: the date and venue of the wedding, what to do about my family in Italy who would be unable to travel to England for the ceremony and how to stretch the inevitable finances attached. We knew that neither of our families would be able to offer any financial support – we would have to save even harder. But we did go to a jeweller together where we chose an engagement ring with a ruby in the centre surrounded by a circle of diamonds. A few months later I also managed to buy Barbara a wrist-watch with a gold strap, which she still wears to this day.

In July I managed to get a few days holiday, and because we had both been working so hard, we decided to forget about saving for a while and go to Paignton in Devon: it was to be the first of very many happy holidays that would shape our life together.

We caught the train to Devon naively hoping to find accommodation, but arrived to find that all the guest houses were full. Barbara suggested asking at a police station in the hope that they might be able to recommend somewhere – preferably not a cell. The friendly police officer on duty took pity on us and suggested that we stay the night at his home. We gladly accepted his invitation and the following morning his wife gave us breakfast. Later in the day we managed to find a couple of single rooms in a guest house in Brixham. We had a wonderful time together and I couldn't help noticing that wherever we went for a meal we were offered "chips with everything". Thankfully, there wasn't a plate of spaghetti Bolognese, English style, to be found.

When I returned to work, I was promoted to chef de rank, which meant that I was entitled to a higher percentage of gratuities: my wages increased from £8 to between £14 and £16, including tips: the extra money couldn't have been more welcome – or more timely.

The exciting part of working at *The Talk of the Town* was – almost literally -rubbing shoulders with the stars, both as entertainers and as customers. I was fascinated to come into contact with names I hadn't heard of in Italy: Sophie Tucker, the Andrews sisters, the Clark Brothers – who were tap dancers – Max Bygraves, Harry Worth, Shirley Bassey, Lena Home, Eartha Kitt and Frankie Vaughan. I also had the honour of serving the King of Jordan and his entourage.

Laying the tables for customers was easy during the week but it was a nightmare at the weekends because all the waiters turned up to collect the cutlery needed for their various waiting stations at the same time. This meant that I had to be there in very good time, especially when famous stars such as Lena Home or Eartha Kitt were performing, as they always attracted a booking of over 750 people. Despite the high profile of the venue, there was never enough crockery and cutlery available – especially for the busy periods. Sometimes we were so desperate for plates, cups and dishes for our own tables that we would hide the crockery in the fire extinguisher cupboards which normally housed a fire blanket, so that there was enough available for us to give to customers. Some time later we found boxes of crockery that had been stashed away as a secret store by one of the waiters, keen to ensure he never ran out.

The charge for a dinner dance and cabaret at *The Talk of the Town* was 37 shillings and sixpence. It was a fixed price whether people had dinner or not – and consequently open to a certain amount of abuse. The waiters could help themselves to food whenever they fancied it – a main course or a starter for example – and even took them home. Unfortunately, the management discovered what was happening and soon put a stop to these easy picnics.

It was a long night for all of us, so when customers outstayed their welcome and sat on until two-thirty or three in the morning, we devised ways of making them realise that it was time to leave. The first was to make a lot of noise when we were washing our cutlery close by and the second was to sprinkle powered ginger around the table to make them sneeze!

Sometimes it wasn't only the waiters who tried a trick or two. Some customers were craftily dishonest and developed clever ways of having a cheap evening's entertainment. They would place a packet of cigarettes or a handbag in an obvious position on the table and then leave without paying the bill, doubtless oblivious to the fact that it was then the head waiter who would be responsible for the cost of their evening.

Fame certainly made no difference to manners, and although the majority of customers were polite, there were notable – and famous – exceptions. One evening I served the famous trumpet player, Eddie Calvert, who, in a haughty manner said "Don't you know who I am?" I was so disgusted at his arrogance that I replied, "No, I've never seen or heard of you." and quietly got on with my job.

Some time later I was invited to share a room with another Italian gentleman in Holborn, near the British Museum – Barbara was relieved that it got me out of Soho. Once he got to know me he told me that he would be away for two or three months at a time, but that he was still prepared to pay his half of the rent provided that I looked after the room well. This gave me the opportunity to do my own cooking and some entertaining on a modest scale. The only snag was that there was no bath which meant I had to use the public baths ten minutes walk away. When my room mate returned, he told me that he was leaving permanently so the room was my responsibility. He also made a helpful suggestion: that Barbara and I might try to find work in Jersey for the summer season, as he had found it particularly lucrative.

Barbara and I set our wedding day for 25th March 1961. In fact we planned to marry twice, once in England and once in Italy. We had decided to be married in a Roman Catholic Church in order to please my family and to this end Barbara took instruction in the Catholic faith every week. As the date of the wedding approached, Barbara went to Westminster Cathedral to obtain permission to be married in a Catholic church. But permission was refused – with only a week to go before the wedding – leaving Barbara terribly distressed.

We discovered later that the refusal was the result of my not attending Mass regularly owing to the irregular hours of my work. I felt hurt by the unsympathetic treatment we received and it turned me against Roman Catholicism.

We were determined not to let red tape and resistance spoil our happiness and

came to an agreement with the local priest who understood our situation and agreed to marry us. Our wedding could go ahead at the Roman Catholic Church in Warlingham on the 25th March 1961 as planned.

We shared the day with several dozen guests including Barbara's family and our friends: celebrations with the Italian side of the family would have to wait.

Barbara told me later, that when she walked down the aisle on the arm of her Grandfather she was so excited that she didn't hear a note of the organ music that was being played. To me she just looked beautiful in her white dress and veil. She arrived at my side smiling broadly and greeted me with the words 'Ciao Mario.'

For our modest reception I had baked a three tier wedding cake and decorated it with pink tinted icing and sugar roses which I also made myself. This time I did not have to carry it precariously across the street on a three legged stool. It was soon demolished, but in quite a different way: some Italian friends who knew nothing about English customs began cutting up the cake and were rather too generous with their portions so that every tier and crumb of the whole cake had soon disappeared. As Barbara's younger brother had been caught lowering food through the window to his friends we could only assume that much of it was pink sugar-iced cake.

At the end of the reception, we went back to Barbara's home to change and get ready for our honeymoon – with Barbara's mother in the car! As we drove away from our crowd of friends and English family, cheering and waving happily, we could hear the sound of tin cans rattling noisily behind the car, proclaiming that we were 'Just married.'

Leslie had agreed to drive us to the airport where we would fly to France before travelling on to Italy for our 'second' wedding celebration. I was secretly quite nervous, not about the romantic implications of the honeymoon-but simply because I had never flown before: I didn't wish to admit this to my new bride. When we boarded the flight we found, to everyone's amusement, that the plane was full of newly married couples all of whom had 'beaten the tax system'.

We were delayed in reaching our Paris hotel, which was near the Sacre Coeur, and were dismayed to find that our double bedded room had been given to someone else. The receptionist saw no problem with this, and simply suggested that we push the single beds together in the room we were offered. We just about managed to avoid plummeting to the floor through the gap and the only thing that marred the passion of our honeymoon was Barbara's discovery that I had brought an inadequate supply of contraceptives!

On the fourth day of our honeymoon we boarded a train for Italy. We stopped in Rimini, which held such special memories for us, staying for two days, before travelling on to Cassano.

My parents had been busy organising our second wedding celebration, the reception for which would be held at the home of my sister, Rosa. We arrived on the Wednesday, with our 'second wedding' set to take place on the Saturday. In order to make people believe that we were not married, my parents had arranged for us to stay in a private room next to my aunt's home and we were told that we should not be seen together until our wedding day. Our only risky public trip was a necessity: we had to sneak away to Bari to collect the cakes for the reception. We went late in the evening to avoid paying the tax on the cakes – a *dazio* – which was then obligatory when carrying any product from one town to another. We felt like smugglers we were as we drove the cakes back to Cassano in darkness. We also knew that we would have to be more careful about offering cakes than wine to our guests at the reception – the cakes were far more expensive.

On the Big Day we dressed in our wedding finery, as if for the first time: somehow the wedding nerves were less the second time around. In the church attached to the convent, about a mile and a half outside Cassano, we repeated our vows in front of our Italian relatives and friends. After the service we drove back into Cassano in an open topped car with my Uncle and Aunt and, as the custom demanded, drove all around the town to show ourselves off to everyone who wished to cheer and offer congratulations. To our great disappointment my younger brother Enzo, who had been instructed to take photographs with Barbara's camera, forgot all about it. Consequently, we have no photographic record of our Italian wedding: perhaps memories are sometimes more vivid.

The reception at my sister Rosa's house allowed those precious smuggled cakes to make their appearance. There was music and dancing and when Barbara and I took to the floor everybody tied us together with streamers, while guests gave us envelopes containing money instead of gifts as we wouldn't be able to carry boxes or parcels back to England.

The following day, after lunch, we opened the envelopes and wrote down how much each guest had given us in order to share and send our thanks: we had been given the princely total sum of around £35. My mother was very interested to see who had given what, saying that she would also make a note – for the future, for when she might have to reciprocate!

As we had arranged to follow up my former room-mate's suggestion of a summer season in Jersey, the ever practical Barbara suggested that we should wait to buy our cutlery on the island, in order to take advantage of the tax perks. I had visions of smuggling spoons in my socks and folding forks into my underwear, but we did as she suggested and are still using that cutlery today!

As it was the custom in Cassano to visit relatives after a wedding to thank them for

Cassano, March 1961.
Mario's mother Alessandra & Father Antonio

their gifts, we embarked on our thankyou tour of the village. Every relative we visited, greeted us warmly and offered us home made liqueur, as was the custom. The words 'home made' and 'liqueur' give little indication of just how strong this alcoholic beverage could be. Because Barbara wasn't used to alcohol she could only manage about three of these drinks, which meant, of course, that I had to drink every one of the glasses subsequently poured for her so as not to be thought rude. In total I must have drunk about fifteen glasses of the less than innocent beverage and needed to hold on to Barbara in order to stay upright for our walk home. In fact, it was a miracle that I could walk at all. Thankfully Barbara could only see the funny side.

We spent several happy days with my family in Cassano, securing at least a few celebratory photographs taken with my parents and my maternal grandmother.

We planned to continue our honeymoon by travelling on to Naples to stay with my brother Franco and his girlfriend Lilli, but when the time came for us to leave, my brother Peppino and my youngest sister, Maria, announced that they intended coming with us. We didn't feel able to say they couldn't, but taking your brother and sister on honeymoon hardly makes for a romantic twosome! To make matters hilariously worse, when we arrived at Franco and Lilli's accommodation in Naples we found that the sleeping arrangements consisted of one large room divided by a curtain with a double bed on each side. There was no choice but for the boys to sleep on one side and the girls on the other.

After a short stay in Naples, during which we went to see Franco and Lilli perform, Peppino and Maria returned to Cassano. Barbara and I travelled on-alone this time, thankfully and finally the honeymoon couple, to Genova.

We stayed with Sig.ra Cordano, Barbara's former landlady, for a few days before leaving by train for Paris. As our flight wasn't until late afternoon we checked in at the airport early and, realising that we had more than the allotted weight of luggage, sat in full view of the airport personnel, stuffing our coat sleeves with

Paris, April 1961. Barbara still celebrating our honeymoon straight from the bottle!!

extra clothing in order to avoid paying the excess!

With our luggage safely stowed we were free to wander around Paris in a carefree – if overdressed – mood. We ended up by the River Seine, eating a baguette and defiantly sending a message to the French by drinking the strong red wine we had brought from Cassano – straight from the bottle. We were in a merry mood, laughing and joking until it was time to return to the airport to catch our flight.

Back in London we went straight to my lodgings in Little Russell Street where we intended to stay until we went to Jersey for the summer season. To our surprise, our landlady had left a beautiful bouquet of flowers to welcome us home, a newly married, very happy, but exhausted couple.

CHAPTER SIX

"I think you ought to know."

I think you ought to know before you go..."

At the end of May, Barbara and I flew to Jersey from Bournemouth to spend the summer season working at the Waters Edge Hotel in Bouley Bay, as arranged. Barbara was to be given the role of hotel receptionist, while I would work as a restaurant waiter. We would be able to work together in a pleasant holiday environment, save on living costs by staying in the hotel's staff accommodation and, most importantly, save as much as possible for our future.

Jersey at that time was not quite the stylish tax haven it is today, but it had a flavour of France and its harbours and beaches provided an alternative for those who wanted to 'Go abroad' without venturing too far out of their comfort zone.

When we arrived at the hotel we met the manager of the restaurant and the personnel manager who briefed us about our work and showed us our rather cramped accommodation. We were told that Barbara was not to be given the position of receptionist as had been arranged, after all. There seemed to be no explanation of this change of arrangement other than the fact that she was my wife and I was a waiter. It was a judgment and decision which incensed Barbara in its injustice, on two counts. Instead, Barbara was offered a position as a laundry assistant. Because we had given up both our jobs and accommodation on the mainland, we had no alternative but to accept, but it was hardly an auspicious start.

We settled down to our work determined to make the best of things, deciding, a few weeks later that if Barbara's job situation could not be changed, we could at least do something to improve our living space. So we moved into the home of a lovely middle aged couple, Mr and Mrs de le Haye, who lived in a house up the hill from the hotel. It meant that we had to walk up that same hill wearily every time we finished our shift, but at least we had our own private and pleasant space away from work. Mr and Mrs De le Haye were more than a landlord and landlady: they became friends who made a huge difference to our stay on the Island. While Barbara and I took the opportunity to see as much of Jersey as possible and enjoyed the beach during our breaks, Mr and Mrs de la Haye drove us all over the island to show us all it had to offer. They also fostered my appreciation of Jersey foodstuffs: milk, cream and even the less than 'dull' potatoes I had been warned about back in Italy.

Barbara's job in the laundry was not without its bright side. She was befriended by the rest of the laundry staff, most of whom were Italian. As Barbara spoke her slowly developing Italian in her conversation with them there were often some hilarious mistakes. When Barbara noticed steam (*fumo* in Italian) disappearing through the laundry window she told the women that *'fume'* meaning a 'river' was flowing through the laundry window, to much hilarity all round!

They patiently taught her how to iron shirts and trousers the Italian way – correctly. I wondered if perhaps those important lessons were the main reason for her change of position. Once those lessons had been learned Barbara was asked to work as a waitress and chambermaid in the Bouley Bay Hotel – a much less steamy option. But because Barbara was new to waitressing she found that there was much to remember: including the basics. One evening, she arrived at the shoulders of her seated customers ready to serve their food from the platters she was carrying. As she lifted the first portion she realised, much to their amusement, that there were no plates on the table!

Our jobs may not have been ideal, but we were happy just working, being together and enjoying the island. We had no idea that we were about to face a sad interruption to that happiness.

One morning, walking down the hill to work we were fooling about as usual and Barbara decided to give her 'little husband' a piggy back ride. Sadly, she didn't realise that she was already pregnant. A few days later she suffered a painful and distressing miscarriage during the night. I felt helpless, but called Mrs de la Haye who was kind and gentle with Barbara and immediately phoned for the doctor. Barbara was admitted to the main hospital in St Helier to recover. The hotel management made little of our situation and were not as understanding as they might have been, asking Barbara to resume work much too soon afterwards. The whole experience made her tired and very depressed. It took her several weeks to get over the miscarriage physically and she began to long for another baby. Beyond our heartache, we simply had to press on and live one day at a time – something we would learn to do increasingly throughout our married life.

The live music at The Waters Edge Hotel – featuring Matt Munroe amongst others – made it a very popular venue for holidaymakers and locals alike. There was also a resident band, whose leader played the accordion. One day the head waiter, Vittorto, encouraged me to play the instrument when he thought no-one was about. Unfortunately, someone *was* about: the band leader. He came in just as I was in mid-flow with a small but appreciative impromptu audience, and was not at all pleased to see someone else using his precious instrument. My exit, stage left, was a swift one.

The dining room at The Water's Edge was broad and airy and furnished with round tables covered with floor length cloths. The space beneath the tables was often used by the waiters to store or hide food in order to speed up the serving process, especially, for some reason, whole roasted chickens-not something health and safety rules would allow today! One evening the head waiter inadvertently accompanied some customers to a table beneath which a cold chicken had been hidden on its serving plate. As the customers sat down and stretched their legs their feet hit the chicken and all was discovered. The head waiter, who was gay, gave a loud scream, flapped his hands in alarm and shrieked "Those naughty boys!" to everyone's great amusement, neatly and swiftly covering up both the chicken and the faux pas with his performance!

Customers were always generous – despite hidden chickens. The tipping system, common to all hotels and restaurants, specified that all tips were put in one box which was shared out at the end of the week. We got to know customers well over the course of their stay and some of those who were particularly generous would give us personal presents as a thank you.

Barbara and I fulfilled our intention of buying a canteen of 'wedding present' cutlery and bought another set for Barbara's brother Leslie, who was due to be married later in the year. Both increased our luggage allowance somewhat and must have amused customs officials, but we had put a good deal of our wedding present money to good use.

We had hoped to save hard while working on Jersey, but because of the employment changes we had faced, we only managed to save about half of the amount we'd planned for. Nevertheless, we put the few hundred pounds we had saved safely away as a deposit for the house which we dreamed of buying some time in the future.

At the end of the season we said our goodbyes to Mr and Mrs de le Haye and flew to Bournemouth where we stayed for a few days break before going first to Barbara's mother's home and then to our new lodgings: an upstairs room in the home of an old lady who liked to be called Auntie Lucy and who insisted on bringing us a cup of tea in the mornings.

I began looking for a job in the Westerham area of Kent and met Tony, a former colleague from the *Talk of the Town,* who suggested that I work with him at a large Tudor style hotel called The Grasshopper Inn. So I started work in the restaurant of The Grasshopper while Barbara found a job preparing the accounts of an electrical shop in Oxted.

After our short stay with Auntie Lucy, we found a small flat of some character on Farley Common, just outside Westerham. The flat was arranged in the former bathroom of a very large manor house and consisted of a bed-sitting room, a small hall and a toilet. Ironically, the bath tub was in the kitchen, covered with a lid which could be used as a work top. Although the flat was full of quirky character, the location was hardly ideal. Whichever direction we took on the Common meant a long walk to and from anywhere: a walk which Barbara often had to do alone and in the dark. But it was our first real home together, we were happy and Christmas was approaching.

We bought a fresh turkey for our Christmas lunch and, as we hadn't got a fridge and it had been snowing, hung it outside on the roof to keep it cold. On Christmas Eve with the vegetables prepared and the ceremony of stuffing about to begin Barbara sent me to rescue the turkey from its chilly roost on the roof. But a hard frost had developed and the window was frozen solid. However hard I shoved and pulled it couldn't be opened: our turkey was marooned on the outside, its hopeful eaters on the inside. I wasn't about to scale the roof in the frost and snow – even for a Christmas turkey. So, lunchtime passed while we waited, and waited, trying the window at frequent intervals. Eventually, when the window began to thaw it shifted a little and the turkey could be hauled in from its icy refuge, its liberation at an end. By the time the poor bird was defrosted and cooked Christmas Day had almost become Boxing Day- but it was worth the wait.

Barbara presented me with a Churchillian sized cigar as a Christmas present, entirely appropriate as Winston's house, Chartwell, was just up the road. But our best Christmas present by far was the knowledge that Barbara was pregnant again. The baby was due later in the summer and we were both delighted by the news. This time we avoided hill climbing and piggy back rides and took extra care of Barbara during her pregnancy to ensure she stayed fit and well.

All was not well at the Grasshopper, however. While at work in the restaurant, I noticed that the chefs were regularly stealing meat to take home. In order to hide this from the management smaller portions would be served to the customers who were oblivious to the profit—laden portion control. I found such blatant dishonesty difficult to cope with. The chef also told me to ask the customers if their meal was satisfactory as I collected their empty plates. If a customer agreed, I was to ask if the chef might deserve a drink as a result. I strongly disapproved of this ruse and after a customer reacted angrily to the suggestion, refused to continue, however unpopular this might make me with the chef.

I also discovered that the restaurant did not declare staff gratutities to the Inland Revenue, as was the legal requirement, and were quite unconcerned about their oversight. Barbara and I went to the local tax office to ask what might be done, but they waved us away saying that they knew all about it. The 'tax on tips' situation was important for us to clarify for more reasons than just promoting honest practice. We wanted to borrow the maximum amount from a building society in order to buy our own home and needed a full statement of earnings to do so. I was heavily relying on Barbara's guidance as I knew nothing of the English system, but we both realised that the only way we could obtain a letter declaring my full income, including tips, was for me to leave the Grasshopper for more honest employers and move back to *The Talk of the Town*.

In the spring 1962, *The Talk of the Town* offered me the position of Wine Butler and Barbara and I found a flat to rent in Streatham Hill, closer to my workplace. By then we had been married a year and were informed by a somewhat stiff and uncompromising letter that an immigration official from the Home Office would be visiting us. He was to interview Barbara to make sure that she was genuinely married to me, that I was responsible for her and that ours was not a marriage of convenience: it caused a few jokes between us. When the official arrived there was a sudden sense of the seriousness of the situation, however amusing it had seemed to us beforehand, and I was sent into another room so that Barbara could be interviewed privately. I'm not sure exactly what she said but she managed to convince him that I shouldn't be sent back to Italy!

Barbara found a job in a letting agency based in Shaftesbury Avenue and worked part time during the day and some evenings, not just for the extra money, but because she didn't wish to be on her own in the flat while I was at work. Although we had begun to look for a house to buy, the landlady in Streatham Hill had quickly realised that Barbara was pregnant and told us that we would have to find other rooms before the baby arrived. It became necessary for us to double our search and look out for rented accommodation at the same time, in case we were unable to find a house to buy. In the late fifties and early sixties, it was very difficult for couples with children to find accommodation of any kind to rent. Immigration was increasing and property boards and notices fixed in windows would

18 Runnymede, Merton Abbey. Mario & Baby Anthony 1962

declare 'Flat to let. No children. Europeans only.' It was a difficult – and often harrowing – search. On one occasion Barbara came home in tears because the staff in the letting agency had been rude to her – simply because she was expecting a baby.

Eventually we found a maisonette we liked and wanted to buy in Merton Abbey, near Colliers Wood. It was priced at £2,800 with a 65 year lease. We mentioned to the Estate Agent that we needed another £300 to reach the deposit of £700, and he quickly offered to arrange a second mortgage through a solicitor whom he recommended. Eager to secure the property, I accepted this offer straight away, not realising that we could have borrowed the money through other channels at a much lower interest rate.

The Merton Abbey maisonette wasn't ideally placed from a travel point of view. The last underground train to Colliers Wood left at about midnight, and as later trains only went as far as Tooting Broadway, I would face a walk of nearly two dark miles after an evening's work. But we felt that the sacrifice would be worth it. We both liked the maisonette; it was on the ground floor and it had a good sized garden – perfect for a new family. More than that it was *ours* and we looked forward to moving in as soon as possible, preferably before the baby was born – but the baby had other ideas.

In the early morning of 11th July, I arrived home from work to find an ambulance parked outside the Streatham flat. Barbara had gone into labour and had dialled 999. So, without even entering the house, I joined her in the back of the ambulance and we set off for Farnborough hospital. Despite the regular pains, Barbara spent the journey telling me that she was convinced that the baby was not going to be born that day and that she expected to be sent home again. Perhaps, subconsciously, she didn't want to take the baby home to where he or she wasn't wanted and longed for it to wait until we were in our own home. But babies never do as they are told: I

The Proud Parents, 1962.
Mario and Barbara with Baby Anthony

watched our first born, Anthony, make his debut at 5pm that afternoon, scowling and howling his way into the world, a pink and writhing, wrinkled bundle. As the nurse cleaned him up and placed him next to Barbara for our approval he looked up at us with unseeing but enquiring eyes as if wondering what all the fuss was about.

Nothing could have prepared me for the elation I felt as our tiny son entered the world. His arrival made me aware of both the wonder of life and the weight of responsibility that was now mine: beginning, unfortunately, with another day's work – almost immediately. Even as he was born, my next evening shift was about to begin and with no sleep and little sustenance, I faced the journey back into London and *The Talk of the Town:* exactly what I felt the birth of my son deserved to become. The hospital staff took pity on me and gave me some tea and strawberries and cream to keep me going, but in reality I sailed through that evening on fatherly joy and adrenalin, telling everyone I met that I was now a father. Anthony had many a toast drunk to him that evening, with most of the wine provided, or at least distributed, by his Dad!

Ten days later we moved into our new home in Merton Abbey with a new baby and a new cooker. After a few sleepless nights, neither of us was entirely sure which of the two would be the most useful in life!

There had been no 'baby shower' for Barbara and no trip to a nursery store in order to buy an expensive layette. Most of our furniture – including a pram – would be given to us over the next few weeks as we settled down to life as parents. Money may have been short, but happiness, albeit tired, bleary eyed happiness, was in plentiful supply: we were a family.

In the Spring of 1963 my cousin Geno visited on his way to Paris, where he was to take up a scholarship in French literature. He stayed with us for a few days to get to know Anthony and we took both of them to Windsor and Oxford by public transport to see the sights. My sister Maria, then in her early twenties, also came from Italy to live with us. Maria made beautiful knitted garments on a knitting machine and had sold them around Cassano. She imagined that if she came to England she would have more opportunities for the sale of her knitwear. Sadly, as we had cautiously anticipated, her business was not a success, so after some searching, she took a job as an au pair with a family in Raynes Park. The family were delighted with her as she did far more than was required and became a much-loved and invaluable member of the family. She stayed in Raynes Park for about seven months before returning to Cassano, during which time Barbara discovered that she was pregnant again: and that the baby would be born in December.

That 'baby' turned out to be 'babies' and the twins – David and Mark – were born on 2nd December 1963: double the trouble and twice the joy. We broke with the tradition of naming them after relatives: a move that was somewhat resented by my family who thought we had named the new additions to their family after actors.

Suddenly Barbara's work as a mother was tripled, she would need some help! We had three little boys under the age of two and were constantly on the go. Every day was a conveyor belt of feeding, changing, bathing and, for us, brief moments of recovering. Barbara's mother helped whenever she could and we got to know our health visitor, Kirstie

Carpenders Park, Herts. Feb 1964. Barbara with new babies, Mark & David

Burnside, whose assurance and practical advice became invaluable. Kirstie was to become a dear friend.

In Italy, my sister Maria had met a young man, Peppino. His family had immigrated to Australia some years earlier and he had returned to Cassano looking for a wife. When he and Maria met they liked each other, he proposed, and they set the date of their wedding for February.

When the invitation to Maria's wedding arrived, we decided that I should take Anthony on his first trip to Italy – Barbara and the twins would stay with friends while I was away. So Anthony and I made our first trip home to Italy together, father and son. It was an 'interesting' trip with a toddler in tow, but a joyous occasion to travel for. My family made a great fuss of Anthony and it was wonderful to see them all again and introduce them to our first little son. Maria and Peppino made

Cassano, Feb. 1964. Maria's Wedding Celebration with: FROM LEFT Franco, Lilli, Friends & then: Peppino, Maria, Little Anthony, Mother Alessandra, Father Antonio, Giuseppes wife Rosa, Saverio, Sister Rosa & Isa

a well-matched couple and spent a few months in Cassano before moving to Australia to join his family in Adelaide.

Life was busy with three small children, especially for Barbara, who found the long hours alone with the boys difficult. But an unfortunate turn of events was to occur which would become something of a blessing in disguise.

One evening at *The Talk of the Town*, as I was serving wine to the customers, one of them handed me a tip of five shillings. I thanked him, and because I was very busy, slipped the half crown into my pocket, intending to hand it to the head waiter for the 'pot' when I could. Unknown to me, one of the senior staff noticed what I had done and wrongly assumed that I intended to keep the money for myself. He reported the incident to the restaurant manager who took me to one side and confronted me. The manager refused to hear my side of the story, despite the fact that another senior waiter spoke up for me, saying that he had done just the same thing on many occasions. The restaurant manager was having none of it and despite my exemplary work record and my reputation for honesty he dismissed me on the spot. I was devastated, not just at the loss of my job, but at the injustice that had caused it. Barbara, however, was not too upset by this news: she was struggling to cope with three babies and was glad to have me at home, even if temporarily.

A few weeks later I heard, through a colleague, about an opening at one of the 'lunches only' Mecca restaurants near Bank station in London. Barbara was delighted when I got the job because it meant that I was at home every evening and at weekends. She would have not only help, but company, at the most demanding time of the day.

But business was not good at the restaurant and after only a few months I was told that regrettably as I was the last person to be employed, I would have to be the first to go. The job had been ideal for us as a family and this time Barbara did not

Anthony in our garden talking to the cat

The boys and friends with an old pram

accept the news of my redundancy favourably. Thankfully I quickly heard of another vacancy at Berner's Hotel in London and went along to ask about it. I was interviewed by the general manager, a very large man who smoked equally large cigars. He looked me up and down a little, and asked a few questions doubtfully, but when he discovered that I had worked at the Waters Edge Hotel in Jersey he was very willing to employ me and asked how soon I could start.

As a lounge waiter at Berner's elegance reigned and I was required to wear tails, a whole new experience for me. There were three shifts with one day off a week. The other lounge waiter, who was Genovese, had already set his own working pattern, and an interesting arrangement with the female kitchen assistant. She was supposed to collect tickets to correspond with the food supplied, but by giving her a backhander the waiter arranged for her to provide the food without the required number of tickets, helping himself to the excess. Once again I was faced with the kind of dishonesty that I found difficult to cope with, but knowing that I must keep my job at all costs, with a new family depending on me, I had little choice but to turn a blind eye.

Barbara, however, found feeding and caring for the boys alone exhausting. She became increasingly exasperated by my long hours at Berner's: hours which included working weekends and even Christmas Day. Ever resourceful, she wrote to the advice pages of a women's magazine to ask how her husband might be able to change his job. They suggested that I should go to the Vocational Guidance Association in Harley Street, where I might take a test to measure my aptitude and interests to see if there was any other type of job I would do well. The test cost twelve guineas – a huge amount of money to us – but we felt it was worth a try as we certainly couldn't go on as we were. So I made an appointment. At the interview I answered a bank of questions covering my skills, abilities, interests and leisure choices. A test score was totalled and cross-referenced and the vocational advisor gave me his conclusions. The test showed that I would be good at jobs which involved art, music and salesmanship.

We were to discover that our twelve guineas was money well invested: it provided the first step to a major change in our lives.

CHAPTER SEVEN:

Perduto Amore (Lost Love.")

"...all of my heart will ever now belong to you..."

Art, music and salesmanship – as recommended by The Vocational Guidance Association – combined well in my new career proposal: to sell musical instruments.

I knew that I would need to complete a course in musical instrument technology, so I found a list of colleges in *Floodlight* magazine and discovered that the London College of Furniture ran the required course, as well as a wide range of other courses linked to musical instruments that I might also choose to take as part of my qualification. I immediately enrolled as a part-time student and was able to use my free mornings from work to attend college three mornings a week. It meant working from mid afternoon until one o'clock in the morning, but Barbara put up with this admirably: the dream of a permanent day job for me lightened every long day she spent alone with the boys.

But after a year and a half I still hadn't achieved the full qualification and I was exhausted, often falling asleep during lectures. I had also become involved with the piano tuning and repairing course, which I found fascinating, but this was taking much longer than I had anticipated. It was obvious that I couldn't go on combining long hours of study with long hours of work, something had to be done.

In a 'while washing up' moment of inspiration, Barbara had an idea. She decided to contact County Hall in London to ask whether I was eligible for a grant to support me in a full time course. Although our home address meant that I didn't qualify via County Hall I was advised to try my own borough and immediately applied to Surrey County Council in Kingston upon Thames. They confirmed that I could indeed apply and an appointment was made for me to see the County Music Advisor who would decide whether my application could be positively supported.

I turned up on the day of the appointment, at the allotted time, with no idea what I would be asked, or what the interview might require. The County Music Advisor worked his way through the usual bank of questions with great seriousness and then asked me why I wished to change my job from that of a waiter to a piano tuner and technician. I gave several reasons, all of them valid and some of them weighty, and in my desperation added, "Besides, I have flat feet. I should never have been a waiter." At last a wry smile appeared on the Advisor's face, but I had no idea whether I had sunk my chances or resurrected them. I was on the point of resigning myself to giving up when, at the very end of the interview he asked me to sing for him. I was totally unprepared: this was an interview for a student grant, not an audition for the Royal Opera House. Nevertheless, I was determined to make the most of my opportunity and burst into the aria from Tosca. The advisor was obviously surprised – but pleasantly so. He sat back in his chair and listened intently with that same wry smile on his face. After a while, he stopped me, congratulated me and told me that I would indeed be eligible for a student grant to support my studies. I was told that the normal course requirement of 5 'O'levels would be overlooked in my case as I had already proved myself a willing student. The tutors at The London College of Furniture were aware that I had left school at the age of eleven and were very keen to help me. I was overjoyed.

Within a week I received a letter confirming that I had been granted a major award for a full—time course in musical instrument technology. Barbara was delighted. She would get her husband back and the boys would see more of their Dad. Even better, I could hand in my notice at Berner's. The reaction of the hotel staff was not so positive: the General Manager told me that I was making a big mistake and that there was not very much money to be made in the music business: "You will soon be asking for your job back." He said.

Well, I haven't asked yet.

Once the jubilant celebrations subsided the financial realities set in. I had previously been earning about £30 a week, but when the grant cheque arrived from the council, Barbara calculated that it would provide the family with less than half that amount per week. She worked out that after paying the essential bills and the mortgage I wouldn't be able to have any pocket money for cigars, drinks or newspapers for the next two years! I felt sure my deprivation wouldn't last *that* long and happily enrolled on as a full time student – cigarless – in the autumn of 1965.

Barbara and I look back on this time as one of the happiest in our married life. I was home by 4.30pm and was able to see much more of the boys who also benefited from my college holidays. At last Barbara had the help and support she needed, we were able to enjoy family life to the full and felt that we were aiming for something new and exciting, *together*.

I thoroughly enjoyed my studies afresh – and awake. The course consisted of piano tuning, action repair, wood work, technical drawing, acoustics and French polishing. We also studied the general knowledge of musical instruments, the relationship of pitch and the tuning of other stringed, piped and wind instruments. Much of my time was spent practising the skills we had been taught while shut away in one of the 'piano cubicles' in college. To begin with there were only eleven cubicles for the sixteen full-time students. This meant first come, first served: I had to leave home early!

The teaching staff at the college were real enthusiasts and more than generous with their time and encouragement.

Mr Roope, the Head of Department, was also the Secretary of the Institute of Musical Instrument Technology (IMIT). A portly man in his sixties, his glasses perched precariously on the end of his nose. He was every bit a scientist and his interests were mainly technical. A true friend and mentor he was enormously helpful to me in so many ways beyond his role as tutor.

Mr White was head of the Tuning Department. He was slim, balding and also wore glasses with very thick lenses above a parrot-like nose: a nose which would move up and down as he talked. He was very particular in his checking of our tuning and his marks were never as generous as Mr Roope's. He also presided over the repair department with Mr Little, also in his sixties, short, bald, and a heavy smoker.

Mr Collier taught technical drawing. He had Mr Little's share of thick white hair as well as his own and always wore a grey suit and waistcoat. He was a studious man with a gentle manner and skilled at his craft, designing and building pianos for John Broadwood and Sons.

Later in the course, Mr Gilby joined the staff. The students found his tuition particularly valuable as he was still 'on the road', doing the job of tuner and technician on a regular basis. He was able to pass on a good deal of practical advice, some of which I still use today.

Mr Roope, I got to know very well. He was so helpful to me that we invited him for supper to say thank you. For some reason it had never occurred to me that he was married, so it was a great surprise when he arrived at our door with a lady in a fur coat. The greater shock was that I had only prepared food for three – and we only had three best plates. Thinking fast, I divided the food into four portions of a smaller, much healthier, size. We ate veal escalope Holstein: a veal escalope topped with a fried egg, with anchovies, melted butter and capers. At the end of the evening, as Mr Roope and his wife left, we were particularly touched when Mrs Roope gave Barbara a pound to take the boys to the zoo.

The following morning, at college, Mr Roope called me into his office. At first I wondered whether the veal had hit the wrong spot. But I was about to benefit from more of Mr Roope's kindness and generosity. "I won't take 'no' for an answer", he told me, taking out his wallet. He withdrew £5 and gave it to me. "Go to Foyle's bookshop straight away," he said "and buy a book on piano tuning and allied arts; a book on acoustics and an Italian/English dictionary." All three were invaluable, but with money tight and priorities focused on the family, I had been unable to afford the luxury of books. So I promptly did as I was told. When Barbara heard the story that evening she was astonished by Mr Roope's generosity.

Far from hitting the 'wrong spot' my veal escalope Holstein must have been memorable, because some time later I found myself cooking professionally at Mr Roope's suggestion. One day the college cook was taken ill and the Principal was desperately searching for someone in the college who would take over the catering on a temporary basis. When he came into to our department with his plea for help, Mr Roope 'volunteered' me saying, "Mario from sunny Italy will do it." I protested: "What about my studies?" But Mr Roope assured me that I would be fine and that on this occasion eating came before education. So I found myself thrown in at the deep end like a contestant on a TV cookery show planning and producing food for 600 students. Five people worked with me in the kitchen, but I had to devise each menu and order the ingredients. I did this for a week and to my complete surprise, received a very welcome pay cheque as a result.

Family life continued to be lively, and during this time, Barbara began suffering the odd blackout .We didn't take them very seriously considering them to be a temporary blip. She was a busy Mum with three adventurous boys: it was understandable that she would become tired and stressed.

We continued to be thankful for the practical help and supportive friendship of our Health Visitor, Kirstie, who spent a good deal of time with Barbara and the boys, as a friend as well as a health professional. Without the modern benefits of disposable nappies it was not unusual to have forty towelling nappies in use, out of use, or pending use, all at the same time! We had a small boiler called a Baby Burco and a pulley line in the kitchen on which we would hang the boys' nappies and clothes, heaving them up towards the ceiling to dry. A lady called Mrs Joyce also came to help Barbara with the boys and we would pay her a small amount. Because she had no grandchildren of her own, she would often spend some of that money on small toys which she would bring for the boys.

I spent a great deal of time making the house childproof as Anthony, David and Mark became budding explorers and climbed everywhere. I fixed vertical bars on the bedroom windows and covered the glass with a clear plastic adhesive to prevent expeditionary accidents.

These were happy, if busy, days with the boys. We especially enjoyed the winter time when the house felt cosy, with its coal fire. At Christmas, as we were short of money, I made the boys wooden toys for presents.

Every evening after their baths they would eat their tea and watch *Pinky and Perky* on our nine inch television set. Then, when they had climbed into their beds I would play the guitar and sing to them. These were very ordinary but truly special times.

By then, the college, which was near Old Street Station in Shoreditch, had acquired another building nearby, where more cubicles and pianos had been installed. At last, almost every student was able to practise tuning at the same time, without quite so much of an early start!

As there were no facilities for refreshment on site, I had the bright idea of providing them myself, in the same enterprising fashion that I had once woven baskets to sell in the telephone exchange. I bought a kettle, some cups and saucers, tea and coffee, and Barbara made some rock cakes. The other students were pleased to be able to buy these as welcome snacks and I made a small profit which gave me some pocket money. Cigars, drinks and newspapers could appear again, in moderation of course.

As far as my studies were concerned, I was soon required to decide in which subject to specialise. My most financially profitable college experience might have encouraged me to swap to catering, but I chose tuning and repairing instruments – mainly the piano. Looking back I am sure I made the right choice.

In order to become a student member of the Institute of Musical Instrument Technology (I.M.I.T.) a student was required to complete a special project on a musical instrument. So I teamed up with another student, Robert (Bob) Williams, from Sri Lanka, or Ceylon, as it was then. Bob came from the capital, Colombo, from where his father, the owner of a piano shop was financing his course.

We decided to study the construction of the Bluthner piano to try to establish why it produced such a distinct, soft and sweet tone. Bob and I enjoyed working together and because he was well educated he took the role of scribe, recording the details of our findings, which was a great help to me. As a result we became good friends, often sharing special events, including a Ceylonese Independence Day celebration held at Kensington Town Hall.

Once Bob and I we were accepted as student members of the IMIT we were able to attend the IMIT highlight of the year – the annual dinner – where the only woman in attendance was the fur coated Mrs Roope in her role as the Secretary's wife. I could just imagine Barbara's reaction to this arrangement: the absence of women in Italian bars and cinemas had been enough to challenge her! So after dinner I approached Mr Roope and commented on the absence of women, suggesting that perhaps our wives should be allowed to attend the event the following year. He looked surprised, but after a pause he agreed. Now, of course, women not only attend the dinner as wives, but enrol on the course, becoming full members of the IMIT.

At the end of the course our research into the Bluthner was published in *Piano World* magazine and Bob and I we were both given associate membership of the IMIT.

As summer was approaching, Bob, Barbara, Bob's girlfriend and I took regular day trips together with the boys. One particular Sunday we went to Chessington Zoo. It should have been an ordinary and enjoyable day, but for Barbara it was filled with niggling concern. We had enjoyed much of the zoo and were approaching the big cats when Barbara suddenly asked me if there were two lions ahead of us or one. We were doubtless somewhat amused at her seeing double, perhaps with twin boys she would be bound to see twin lions? But Barbara was silent and confided in me later that she really had seen double. As is so often the case, we pushed any concerns we may have had to one side. Life was good, what could spoil it for us?

As I was at home for the whole of the long summer holidays of 1966, Barbara took a temporary job in the accounts department of the Abbey National Building Society in Baker Street. It gave us all a little extra money, and Barbara some much needed independence.

On the day of the England v. Germany World Cup Final match Barbara went to Wimbledon to have hair done, as most sensible women would during a football game. It was something she had not been able to do for a long time and she was amused to find that the streets – if not the hair salon – were completely deserted.

That same weekend Barbara's mother came to visit us. She planned to stay for a few days to baby-sit, as I had promised to take Barbara out for dinner on the Monday evening as a treat and to give her the opportunity to dress up and show off her new hair-do. Barbara went off to work happily that Monday morning – her second week at work – and I arranged to meet her at the staff entrance in the evening. We were both excited at the prospect of a dinner alone together.

At the end of the day I stood at the staff entrance as arranged and waited happily, but there was no sign of Barbara. I grew increasingly concerned, wondering if perhaps I was waiting at the wrong entrance, until eventually a lady hurried towards me looking anxious. She asked me if I was Mr Campanale and when I said that I was she told me that Barbara had gone to Maida Vale Eye Hospital in Marylebone as she was seeing double. I immediately remembered the twin lions at Chessington and knew something must be very wrong.

I went straight to the hospital where I was told that Barbara had been rushed to the National Hospital for Nervous Diseases in Queen's Square. It was there that I finally found her, in a neurology ward, looking pale and tired. She had already had the back of her head shaved by the nurses in preparation for an investigation the following morning. There were mutterings and discussions amongst the attending staff with suggestions of brain tumours and surgery, while I was advised to return home to rest and to visit the following day.

There was nothing I could do but go home on the train to tell the boys that their Mum was in hospital.

As I travelled home – numb and anonymous amongst dozens of passengers going about their ordinary everyday lives while ours was being so horribly shaken – I remained in a state of shock. I had heard almost nothing about brain tumours: they were something from another world; a world where bad things happened to other people. I knew neither what to think nor what to expect. I daren't think ahead or consider the possible consequences, each was too painful an exercise and one which led me down a pathway of fear and bewilderment.

The following day I returned to the National Hospital, by which time Barbara's head was completely shaved. We tried to laugh at the waste of an expensive World Cup hairdo, but our deep anxiety was barely hidden from one another.

We were told that the investigation to locate the tumour would involve drilling three holes in Barbara's skull and injecting coloured fluid through her neck so that so that the dye would show up on a brain scan. It was an unpleasant thought and an unpleasant procedure, but somehow the 'not knowing' was worse.

The following Wednesday when the results had been analysed, we were told that a tumour – a menginioma – had been found and that it was, thankfully, benign. Benign it may have been, but it was, nevertheless, causing trouble and would have to be removed: as by this time Barbara had completely lost her sight. The surgeon, Sir Wyley McKissack, and his team explained in great detail what they were going to do and how they would operate. He said that he was confident that the operation would be success. We could do nothing but attempt to share his faith and confidence.

The surgery the following day took eight hours and when I visited Barbara that evening her head was swathed in bandages and her pretty face was swollen and very blue. The boys were allowed to see her within a few days, but as she was sedated she wasn't able to speak to them. Anthony, in his bewildered disappointment, said that he couldn't see any reason for them being there as Mum was fast asleep. But she told us later that there had been a very good reason for the boys being there: she had been able to hear them chattering and moving about and this had given her the motivation to get well.

The operation was the success we had so hoped for. About a week later Barbara's vision returned and she was able to see the boys again. In fact, she couldn't stop looking at them.

As Barbara recovered, the hospital almoner visited her to discuss the issues related to her discharge. The almoner asked about the conditions at home, whether I was working, how many children we had and what our living arrangements were, in order to give advice on how best to cope. Barbara told her that Anthony was four years old, that the twins were two and a half and that I was studying at home so that I could look after the children: ours was a far from easy family situation. As a result, we were told that the hospital would pay my fare each time I visited Barbara. They also sent me a cheque for £60 towards the expenses we had – and would – incur and suggested that I write to the council to see if they would give me an additional grant as I was unable to work: we later received a cheque for £40.

We sensed that we were being well looked after – in more ways than one.

Whilst in hospital Barbara had several 'out of body' experiences. She felt that she was being lifted towards the ceiling from where she was able to look down at herself in bed. Far from being frightening, these experiences gave her a feeling of calm. She also had visions of walking through a lovely garden and approaching a gate where she was met by an old lady who sent her back, saying that it was not her turn to go through yet.

As she lay in bed one day she experienced a feeling of warmth moving from her feet right up through her whole body, accompanied by a sense of intense peace. A few days later when she was visited by the Methodist chaplain from the hospital she told him this story. Far from being sceptical, he said he was delighted to hear about her experience, explaining that he and his prayer group had been praying for Barbara at that exact time.

As the days passed, Barbara began to re-learn how to walk and read and co-ordinate her movements, it was essential to retrain her brain to perform the most basic tasks. It was a long, slow process for which she saw two or three therapists every day.

Several weeks later she was sent from the National Hospital to a convalescent home in Finchley. It was not an ideal placement, as the majority of the patients suffered from epileptic fits and it distressed Barbara to see them fall to the ground and fit. But she stayed in convalescence for three weeks continuing with her painstaking and exhausting therapy. I faced an hour's journey each way by under-ground to visit her- travelling between Colliers Wood and East Finchley – and had to make arrangements for the children to be looked after while I was away. But I could hardly complain: my journey was far less complex and arduous than Barbara's.

The day Barbara finally returned home was a triumphant one. The boys were delighted to have their Mum back, even if they failed to understand just how easily she would have to take life for a while. It didn't always help to have th e lively boys jumping onto her lap or demanding her attention! But there could be no complaints – she was home, and that was what mattered. Barbara was supplied with a wig by the hospital but chose not to wear it. It was scratchy and stiff and looked nothing like her own lovely hair. She preferred to wear an artfully arranged silk head scarf instead: it looked rather elegant!

In September of 1966, I returned to college to carry on with my studies, and although in November it became clear that I would have to repeat a term to make up for the time I had missed, an extra grant was paid to support me through the additional months.

After Christmas, one of my tutors suggested that I should try to gain practical experience of selling instruments by working in a piano workshop in one of the large stores. So I worked in Heals in Tottenham Court Road for a fortnight. At the same time, a lady who lived nearby sometimes asked for a student piano tuner to tune her piano and Mr Roope chose me. It was excellent real-life experience and to my delight the lady concerned offered me a meal, as well as the required tuning fee of five shillings.

As the end of my college course approached, Barbara suggested I write to piano companies and councils applying for a job. I obtained a list from the library and wrote letters to twelve piano shops and county councils. Out of those twelve I was offered seven jobs, including positions at Morley's of Lewisham and Maxwell's of Wimbledon.

I turned down the job at Morley's, even though the salary was very good. I had discovered that I would have to wear a striped suit, carry an umbrella and wear a bowler hat! This did not suit my sense of style, or my image. I was an Italian-not an English city gent!

Maxwell's of Wimbledon offered £16 a week – the same amount as my student grant at that stage. But for that modest amount I would be required to tune twenty pianos a week and work every Saturday. When I told the staff at the college about my interview at Maxwell's and the terms of employment, Mr Roope was horrified. He felt obliged to write to inform them that they were underpaying their employees. He was a man of results: those employees received a swift and unexpected pay rise!

The final of my seven interviews was at Squires of Ealing. After completing a tuning on a Steinway grand piano, which was situated in the shop window, they said they would let me know, as the company already had its full complement of staff. But then rather a miraculous thing happened. A few days later, a wealthy young couple visited Squires with the intention of buying a grand piano. They tried the Steinway grand in the window and said they would buy it, but only on condition that whoever had tuned the piano previously should carry on tuning it for them in the future. Squires were so impressed by this that they decided to employ me immediately. We agreed that I would begin working for them part-time, as soon as I qualified.

At the end of January, my course at last completed, I was presented with my college certificate of qualification and an award for 'The Most Outstanding Student of the Year' with a prize of five guineas. I was overwhelmed. My fantasy was to spend the prize money on an easel and some oil paints so that I could sit by the river and quietly paint – the only part of the vocational advice given to me that I had yet to fulfil, after all. Unfortunately, Barbara didn't agree with my fantasy plan and the money quickly went into the general housekeeping fund. Any artistic leanings which were left unfulfilled would need to be channelled into my new job: as a fully qualified piano tuner and technician.

"*It's Time to Smile!*"

I began working for Squires in February 1967 and was paid via commission, with travel expenses, holiday pay, and a promise of a pension scheme and further commission after a year's employment.

In the first few weeks I was sent out to tune pianos in the Ealing area, travelling by public transport. I encouraged three of those customers to buy new pianos from the shop. As a result, my commission rate was increased five fold, which initially caused great resentment among the other sales staff. But as my relationship with them improved we managed to work together to bring more people into the shop, selling more pianos and commissioning more repair work.

As a family we moved to Beards Hill Close in Hampton, because we wanted to live near Kingston upon Thames, but travelling by public transport for work was still very time-consuming. I decided to take driving lessons in the hope that Squires would supply me with a car. I finally passed at the fourth attempt and we began thinking about buying a car of our own.

Barbara found a job at the William Harris Bacon Company to help us to save for auto-mobility. She worked in the accounts office four hours a day and was given a very handsome hamper at Christmas – literally bringing home the bacon! The bacon was eaten, we saved hard, and in May 1968 we bought a Ford Anglia from Barbara's brother Leslie for £90. It would turn out not to be quite the dream car we had hoped for, but it was a start.

Our first Grand Tour by car was to a holiday camp in Hayling Island for our summer holiday. As my guitar had travelled with us, Barbara encouraged me to take part in the talent competition. I sang 'O sole mio' in the style of Elvis Presley's "It's Now or Never" and Malaguena in Spanish-and won first prize: a free week's holiday for one week for two people at the same holiday camp! Anthony won a cup for the loudest cry in the Tarzan Cry competition – I could have predicted that at his birth – as well as a prize for singing 'Non Ho l'eta', in Italian: the song which won the Eurovision Song contest that year.

So, the following October we returned to Hayling Island for our free holiday and, more importantly, to take part in the semi-

David, Anthony & Mark being Police boys complete with "slippers" and "machine guns"

final of the talent competition. I decided to sing the same songs, coming second, while the winner sang 'Delilah', made popular by Tom Jones.

While we were enjoying our break, the Anglia decided to begin its rebellion. The car park attendant at the holiday camp kindly offered to wash the car, but as he did so his hand went right through the wing uninvited: Leslie had patched it up with fibreglass. On our rainy return journey I discovered that the windscreen wipers had joined in the revolt and flatly refused to work. I had to put my hand out of the window frequently en route to clear the windscreen.

Hayling Island October 1968. Sunshine Holiday Camp. The boys having a good time.

In exasperation I decided to trade in the Anglia and approached Mr Squire for a loan to buy a better car. He agreed to lend me £360, interest free, to be paid back on a monthly basis and offered to pay me mileage when I used the car for work. I chose a Bedford Beagle estate car from a garage in Wimbledon and couldn't wait to drive it. As the paperwork was completed and I inspected my gleaming new motor the salesman spotted the old Anglia on the forecourt and exclaimed with some amusement "Whose old heap is that?" Of course, I hadn't a clue.

The boys were growing fast and once they were old enough, started school locally, although we soon discovered that the Head Teacher encouraged a very informal style. It was the late sixties and 'learning by discovery' and 'integrated days' were the norm in primary schools across the country. Each method may have had its merits but our bright and lively boys needed a little more direction. As they were not progressing with their reading, we found a tutor who offered to teach them to read 'in a month' – and she did exactly that.

Gradually, as a family, we got to know neighbours and made good friends in Hampton and particularly at St Mary's Church. The twins joined the church choir, later passing an audition to join the Chapel Royal choir at Hampton Court Palace, but preferring to stay at St Mary's where they too had made so many friends.

Barbara's friend Ula was a member of the chorus at The Royal Opera House, and suggested that the boys might like to take their singing one stage further -literally. To that end they entered, and passed, an audition to be village boys in a Verdi opera – "The Force of Destiny" – at the Royal Opera House, Covent Garden. They were collected by car twice a week for the six week run and made very sure they were noticed. One day, during a full costume rehearsal, Colin Davis was conducting the chorus when there was a lot of giggling on stage. Distracted, he hit his baton on the lectern, stopped the orchestra in full flow and cried "What on earth is happening over there?" Suddenly, amongst a considerable amount of ruffling and swishing, the twins emerged from beneath the underskirts of the ladies of the chorus to shrieks of amusement – and not a little notoriety for the twins!

Anthony's preference meanwhile was the quieter, less sensational, membership of the local cub-scout group.

In 1970, Barbara's sister Helen suffered a severe nervous breakdown. She recovered gradually, and as her health began to improve we invited her to travel to Italy with us, hoping that a holiday would help her convalescence.

Cassano 1969. Our fields, Malatesta. Nonno Antonio moving the mule to pull the traino (cart) to go back home with Barbara, myself and the boys with her sister Helen

In Switzerland, en route to Italy, we took a short cut through the mountains -the most stressful 30 kilometres that I have ever driven – but eventually reached Locarno safely. We stayed in accommodation arranged by Franco and Lilli – now married, with a baby, Sergio – as they were performing there. We drove on to Lugano together and found delightful rooms in a guest house. There, I discovered a piano on the landing which was terribly out of tune (spotting out of tune pianos while on holiday would become something of an occupational habit for me.) I explained to the landlady that I was a professional tuner who would do the job well and she offered to forgo all our accommodation expenses in return. Franco, astonished at the deal, showed a sudden interest in my new job and began to consider how he might combine it with being a musician!

The following day we continued our drive south to spend several days in Rimini, before staying with my parents in Cassano. They were very kind to Helen who enjoyed her holiday and looked and felt well: so very young, in fact, that everyone called her Signorina. She was to return home rejuvenated.

Travelling back through France en route to Calais we stopped at a small town with three hungry boys on board. Our funds had depleted somewhat, so I went on my own to a cafe to ask if we could be provided with some food, explaining that I only had the equivalent of about £1 in French currency. The proprietor generously agreed and asked me to bring in the family. They served us an enormous tureen of delicious soup and an extra long French loaf making a huge fuss of us all. Despite eating their fill, the boys were very eager to get back to Dover so that they could enjoy a typical English bacon and egg breakfast.

As we travelled through France, Barbara had begun to feel neuralgic pain in her left cheek which continued when we arrived home. Our GP was adamant that the pain was not caused by the return of the tumour but gave Barbara such strong pain killers that she collapsed. The dosage was halved, but it didn't bring relief. So I contacted the National Hospital for Nervous Diseases, where Barbara had benefited from her earlier surgery, and asked if Barbara could be readmitted for examination. The medical team agreed to do a brain scan and we waited anxiously for the results, hoping that the GP had been right all along. But the slides showed that the tumour had indeed re-grown: sadly, our GP could not have been more wrong. We were devastated.

The doctors at the National explained that they could not operate because the second tumour was deeper than the first. Instead, they referred Barbara to the Royal Marsden Hospital in Sutton to undergo a series of radiotherapy treatments in an attempt to shrink the mass. Careful measurements of the site of the tumour were taken and a special mask was made to protect Barbara's face from the radioactive beams. She underwent thirty doses of radiotherapy – one on almost every day – each lasting a minute. She became adept at adopting exactly the same position on the radiotherapy table each time and learnt to stay very still so that the treatment hit exactly the right spot. The treatment was painless, if tiring, and its ominous buzzing sound reminded Barbara that the tumour was being well and truly 'zapped'. For the first twenty days she was an out—patient but towards the end, as tiredness and some soreness of the skin set in and final treatments became more focused, it was necessary for her to be admitted to finish the course.

There is always a great deal of waiting involved in any hospital treatment, so to

fill the time as the treatment progressed, Barbara began knitting three Arran jumpers: one each for the boys and a plain one for me. They gave her something to aim for and she was determined to finish them. She managed to complete the three for the boys by the end of the treatment but on her return home found it impossible to concentrate for long enough to finish mine. She obviously needed something more than an Aran sweater and knitting needles to motivate her.

St Mary's Church, Hampton 1973, Mark and David choir boys

Before the discovery of the re-grown tumour, we had been saving for some time to go to America to visit relatives. But when the doctors heard about our plans to travel so far they were concerned that Barbara was not well enough to cope with the journey. She was very weak as she had lost her appetite and would eat only citrus fruit .The doctors told her that they were worried about her health and advised her not to travel. But Barbara was made of stronger stuff and had made up her mind to go, not least because the insurance company had made it clear that they would not refund the travel costs due to Barbara's ongoing medical condition. With such practical and financial motivation, Barbara's appetite began to improve, she grew stronger, and our trip to America seemed a very real probability.

Boston August 1971. Barbara & Mario with the boys, cousin Mary, Geno's sister

In August that probability became a certainty and we set off for our three week holiday in the States. Barbara – who had lost the hair above her forehead – looked very like Queen Elizabeth I, with the determination to match.

There were no direct flights to Boston, so we flew to New York to be met by my cousins Geno and Lorenzo before making the four hour onward drive to our American 'home'. We were given a tremendous welcome by the family and discovered that arrangements had been made for the boys to go with their American cousins to a day camp, where one of my cousins was a supervisor: it was here that the boys learned to swim.

Hunger and boredom were never likely on that holiday. We were served pound weight steaks at a local steak house – and provided with a doggy bag in order to finish them for breakfast the next day. We went to Cape Cod; saw the JF Kennedy Memorial and visited a Chinese restaurant in China Town where the boys wouldn't try the strange food and were suddenly 'not hungry' but requested an omelette as soon as they were 'home'. While the boys were at camp, Geno showed us the Boston area, including the living museum in Plymouth, Massachusetts, the landing point of the Pilgrim Fathers.

It was a wonderful holiday – and Barbara thrived. We even spent time considering whether we might immigrate to the States and enquired about a job as a piano tuner at various piano shops in Boston. The manager of one of them offered me a job at 400 dollars a week and said that if I couldn't make it a permanent arrangement would I stay for three months in order to help him out? Although the offer was tempting, after talking with Geno we decided against the move. The first consideration was the boy's education and Geno thought that an English education would be better for them. We also had to accept that Barbara would never be able to get medical insurance. It was, of course, the right decision.

On our return to England Barbara visited the Royal Marsden for a check up where the doctors were amazed at the positive change in her condition. It was clear that the stimulus of new places and the kindness of loved ones had worked wonders. We could only hope and pray

In March 1973, Barbara called me at work to say that she had just received some news from Italy – my father had suffered a serious heart attack. As practical as ever, she quickly arranged some Italian currency and booked a flight for the same afternoon. Luckily, our friend Ula was visiting and she offered to stay with Barbara to help with the boys. So I went to Italy.

My father died after a short stay in hospital. We paid for the ambulance to take his body home the same day, where we dressed him for his funeral which was arranged within 24 hours, according to custom.

He had always been a man of few words, proud, hardworking and quietly protective of his family. I remembered him collecting me from school and wrapping me in his cloak against the cold and lifting me onto his lap for stories. His quiet presence was now gone from our lives.

The following spring, my brother, Franco's group was disbanded and he and Lilli had to decide quickly what they should do. As there was no likelihood of him finding permanent employment in the musical world in Italy, I suggested that he stay with us for a few weeks to see if he could find a job in England. At least this time I wouldn't face getting into arrears with the rent in order to help him!

We knew an Italian musician who told us that the Villa Dei Cesari restaurant in London needed a saxophone player. Barbara accompanied Franco to the audition where he met the Italians in the band, got on well with them and was offered the job. He returned to Italy to make arrangements for a new life abroad and after a few days drove Lilli and Sergio back to England. They stayed with us while they looked for accommodation, and were able to pick up at least a little English, get used to the currency and begin to understand a few of the stranger English customs. Still remembering my own struggle and bewilderment

Surbiton, Surrey. Barbara's brother Leslie with our three boys, his three children and Barbara's sister Helen's two boys

from years before, they had my sympathy and support!

We then heard of an Italian family who were due to vacate their ground-floor maisonette in Hampton Hill. It was in a good position close to public transport and schools and seemed ideal. Franco and Lilli moved in, and soon after, Sergio was able to start school.

It was all change for other members of the family too. By this time, my younger sister Maria – who had emigrated to Australia – had been busy. She had made arrangements for my sister Rosa, her husband Saverio and their family, to join her in Australia, along with my younger brother Enzo, his wife Lina and their two sons. There were now more members of the family living outside of Italy, than in.

In November it was time for us to be on the move again – not quite as far as Australia – but 'up the road', to Barlow Road, in Hampton: a quiet, leafy street lined with lilac and apple trees. We have lived there happily ever since.

Squires continued their promotional concerts and, on one occasion, held a recital in Ealing Town Hall in front of an invited audience. Once again, I was involved – ever the performer! The day before the concert, I innocently announced to the staff that I was going to exhibit myself in the Town Hall. There was a stunned silence, before one of the girls loudly but light-heartedly exclaimed, "You dirty old man!" The rest of the staff disappeared behind the counters to chortle their embarrassment while someone explained to me exactly what it was that I had said. I had translated direct from the Italian in which it is perfectly correct to use the word 'exhibit', meaning to display one's talents. I vowed to try to remember these further subtleties of the English language which I had still obviously yet to master fully.

Some of the staff at Squires were members of the Ealing Dramatic Society and were rehearsing for Neil Simon's comedy 'Barefoot in the Park'. As one of the characters, called Velasco, was Latin American they asked if I would take on the role. I had never acted before, so it was a new challenge which Barbara encouraged me to tackle, even though it meant rehearsing in Ealing two or three nights a week. My character was required to flirt with an attractive lady – how hard could that be? But at one of the first rehearsals the producer kept asking me to show some emotion, whereas I was standing stiffly doing no more than simply reciting my lines. "Mario!" the producer cried, in desperation, "You are supposed to be a hot blooded Italian! Can't you flirt?" I realised then, that when I had first arrived in England, Barbara had gently told me that I shouldn't be so demonstrative. As a result I had gone to the other extreme-even on stage! Composing and playing the incidental music for the production was more comfortable: it involved a lot less flirting! Yet despite my initial shyness, the production went well, and with some excitement Barbara brought the boys along to watch their famous actor father on stage – trying very hard to flirt.

For some time, incidental musical melodies had been coming into my head which I would play on the piano. Because I couldn't read or write music, I was unable to write them down, so Ula introduced me to Conrad Leonard who had been a conductor and composer all his life. He happily agreed to record my tunes, turning them into sheet music, in exchange for my tuning his piano. My friendship with Conrad was to be a long and delightful partnership of composing and manuscript writing.

The first tune I entitled *'Lost Love'* – and Conrad wrote lyrics for it. At the time I was tuning the piano for the pop group The Tremoloes and when they heard my tune they offered to record it as a demonstration disc. Soon after, another melody came to me and I played it at one of Squire's Christmas parties asking my colleagues to suggest a title. One of the directors suggested calling it *'Mario's Theme'* and Conrad subsequently noted and audio-recorded both *'Mario's Theme'* and *'Lost Love'*. Peter Moore, the conductor and arranger, suggested that I send the tape of *'Lost Love'* to Musac, a subsidiary of Rediffusion. I heard nothing for several months but then sent them *'Mario's Theme'* and within three weeks had received a contract for both titles, with a request for a manuscript for recording use. A little later, they sent me a copy of the orchestration of both pieces. Hearing the professional performance of my music for the first time was thrilling for all of us.

As a result of the publication, I was automatically made a member of the British Academy of Songwriters, Composers and Authors, as well as of the Performing Rights Society. Over thirty songs later, I have the satisfaction not only of royalties, but of knowing that my music has been played all over the world. Each year I am invited to the Gold Badge and Ivor Novello awards at some of London's most prestigious venues. There I can meet fellow songwriters and artists and feel every inch the star!

As I usually play one of my own pieces after completing the tuning of a piano, customers often asked me where they could obtain the music, so I arranged for all my titles to be compiled and printed in a book – all 300 copies were enthusiastically bought by customers. It still gives me great pleasure to know that they enjoy playing my music.

Around this time I was asked to develop something of a musical and professional sideline. For a short period I taught evening and daytime classes for The London College of Furniture, teaching alongside my regular tuning and repair work. Although I enjoyed it, I preferred the independence and variety of tuning to the timetables and tutoring of the classroom.

One of the most enjoyable parts of travelling around London to tune and repair pianos was simply meeting people – often in unpredictable circumstances.

On one occasion I visited an Armenian family and carrying the large briefcase of tuning tools and felts that I always had with me, I was greeted by the husband whom I had never met. He seemed rather anxious and showed me up to the bedroom where, unknown to me, his wife lay ill. As I followed him up the stairs listening to his description of symptoms and concerns, it dawned on me that he thought I was the doctor! When we reached the bedroom, his wife, who recognised me as the musician rather than the medic, burst into almost uncontrollable laughter. Recovering from her laughter she began to feel much better. She told her husband to cancel the doctor and joined us for Turkish coffee downstairs.

A piano tuner colleague was sent to tune the piano of a gentleman who lived in a basement flat . The gentleman made arrangements for access to the flat in advance and explained that although he was not able to be there himself, his dog would be. My friend let himself into the flat, located the instrument – and the dog – and tuned the piano as the dog lay in easy companionship and approval. However, when he tried to leave, the dog showed that he would prefer him to stay, refusing to allow him to open the door, barking and growling his disapproval. The poor piano tuner was left with little choice but to climb out of the window, up the railings to street level and onto the pavement. Just as he did so a policeman walked past and promptly accused him of burglary. It took some time for my colleague to convince the officer that his story "I really *am* a piano tuner escaping from a customer's dog" – was entirely true.

For some reason, embarrassment often goes with piano tuning territory: I was once asked to tune the piano of a female customer who lived near Godalming. She explained that her house was aptly named 'Singmore', but that the 'g' had recently dropped off the sign and was yet to be replaced. Consequently, I approached the house – and the customer – with some caution, wondering what my visit might entail!

Sadly, the job often highlights the desperation of human loneliness. There have been many occasions when I have been asked to tune pianos belonging to very lonely people who just wanted to speak to someone – the tuning of their piano was irrelevant. One of my colleagues was called to the home of an elderly couple only to be told that they didn't own a piano but just wished to talk to him. They assured him that he would be paid in full.

Almost every year we would travel to Italy by car as a family, and as the boys grew those journeys would become more eventful, due largely to the very nature of our passengers and, more often than not, their appetites! By the time they were in their late teens they began looking for a little more excitement on the way and suggested we try an alternative route via Belgium, Luxembourg, Germany and Austria, the latter simply to try Black Forest Gateau.

As I wanted the boys to understand the cultural life of Europe as well as eat the culinary side we did try to broaden their itinerary, on one occasion by staying in Salzburg to visit's Mozart's home!

So on that same holiday we drove to Cremona where Stradivari violins were made and visited an exhibition of Stradiveri, Guarnieri, and Amati violins.

When we heard that Pavarotti was singing the lead role in Il Travatore at the Arena in Verona we were determined to go. As we couldn't book tickets at a distance we set off on the 100 mile plus journey to Verona to secure them. We arrived just as there had been a bomb scare and were caught in chaotic queues of traffic. There was pandemonium in the streets and drivers were mounting the kerbs in their cars in a panic to get away from the centre. By the time we got to the Arena it was eight o'clock, with the opera due to begin at nine. I explained our predicament to the attendant at one of the entrances and he allowed us to go in for a payment of 20,000

Covent Garden Opera House, February 1982.
The Maestro Pavarotti with Mark, David, Barbara, Anthony and Mario

lire. We quickly bought some panini and mineral water and hired five cushions – a necessity on the cold stone seats. The Arena was brimming with expectation and excitement. It was an amazing sight to see 25,000 people assembled in one place, all of them holding tiny lighted candles, which flickered in the gathering dusk.

Hush fell and Pavarotti took to the stage with a cast of three hundred. He gave an outstanding performance which the BBC filmed for a biographical documentary: we made a note to watch it. After Verona we travelled South to Rimini and then on to Cassano for the rest of our holiday, but once we were home again, we remembered the filming and avidly watched *'The Man with the High C's'*. Anthony audio taped it and enjoyed it so much that he listened to it while studying for the A level exams that would enable him to go to Exeter University. After he received his place, he wrote to Pavarotti thanking him for the programme and telling him how much the music had helped him to study. To his surprise Pavarotti replied, thanking Anthony for his letter and encouraging him to continue with his studies. Some time later I too wrote a letter to Pavarotti – in Italian. He replied saying that he was due to be at Covent Garden the following February to sing in *'Un Ballo in Maschera'*, and invited us to meet him in his dressing room at the end of the performance.

So we met up and were photographed together while he complimented me on my three sons. Pavarotti explained that he has three daughters – much more trouble for a Father!

The boys had taken their 'O' levels at Teddington Boys school in the late 1970's, after which Anthony chose to go to Richmond College to study Physics and Maths before later applying to Exeter and – a year later – the twins started their studies at

Kingston College. David was told that if he worked very hard he had the ability to apply for Oxbridge. He was eventually called for interview at University College, Oxford, and offered a place. David rang to tell me the news while I was tuning the piano of a customer in Gerrards Cross. When she asked me the cause of my obvious delight, I explained and she went rather quiet. 'How can this be?' she asked, 'When my friend's son went to Eton he gained three 'A' levels, but he didn't get into Oxford!' Her attitude towards me changed from that point and she even went on to ask my advice about her own son's university applications. Mark, meanwhile, had chosen to go to York University. He had been required to learn a second language for his course, so spent time in Faenza before starting his studies. Unfortunately the Italians he stayed with spoke excellent English and he returned home having learnt very little Italian, but the University still welcomed him.

We suddenly found that all of our boys had left home and Barbara was sitting in an empty nest which needed to be filled. In September, we were asked by friends in Faenza if we were able to give lodgings to Domenico, their daughter's boyfriend, to enable him to learn English. Barbara was delighted as they got on very well. She had someone to care for and nurture, saying, 'I've lost three sons but I've gained a new one.' Domenico also provided company and consolation for Barbara when her mother was diagnosed with lung cancer – later dying, in December 1982. She had been a heavy smoker, and had even sent me packets of cigarettes while I was on National Service. Domenico gave Barbara someone to care for when I wasn't around and enabled her to continue being 'a Mum' even as she recovered from the loss of her own.

A few months later Barbara began to notice the return of the neuralgia-like pains in her face, so we went back to the National Neurological Hospital in London where she was admitted for a week of tests. When the results were analysed we were told that the tumour had re-grown, but that once again it was impossible to operate as it was too deeply placed and there would be a risk of paralysis or loss of sight during surgery. As Barbara had already received large amounts of radiotherapy to the head, there was nothing more that could be done. We were advised to 'live for the day': those four words became our philosophy for life.

To give us hope, our dear friend and neighbour, Glenys, suggested that Barbara should visit Benskins, a Christian Healing centre near Hastings.

We visited Benskins on the 1st of May 1983, driving down with Barbara feeling nauseous and depressed. When we arrived we joined in with

Bari, August 1980. David, Anthony & Mark with Zia Faostina & son Ciccio outside his railway home

Acquaviva Delle Fonti, July 1978.
Barbara with Signora Cafaro on her Terrazzo

hymns and prayers in the sanctuary and were then taken into a small side-chapel where one of the directors, Jennifer Stacey-Marks, began laying her hands on the heads of people who were kneeling at the altar rail. Afterwards, most of them – including Barbara – appeared to faint and were caught by people standing behind them, who gently lowered them to the floor. Within a few minutes they had all recovered and were invited to have a cup of tea and biscuits in the main room. I realised that even at this point Barbara seemed brighter and more alert. On the journey home we stopped for supper as she was suddenly very hungry and not at all nauseous. The following morning Barbara got up, went downstairs and started to do some paperwork – something she hadn't been able to do for months.

When we returned to The Royal Marsden the medical team and even the hospital car driver hardly recognised Barbara because she looked so well. She explained that she had been to Benskins and told them what had happened. They had to accept that there could be no other reason for her dramatic recovery.

We decided to continue to 'live for the day' and to travel worldwide together as much as we could, while we could. It is a decision that we have never regretted.

Cassano, July 1980. Franco, Peppino, Mamma
& Mario outside her home

England, 1982. Barbara, Mario
and the boys with Marina

CHAPTER EIGHT

Bunasera Venezia (Say Hello to Venice.")

There is a song that we always sing, in every springtime in Venezia;
A song of love, of wonderful nights, romantic delights,
when we were young...

Inevitably, Italy has become the most important part of our 'Live for the day' travel.

In May 1983 Domenico – Barbara's surrogate son – and Manuela invited us to their wedding in Italy. A fabulous champagne reception and five course meal belied the 'laid back' approach of bride and groom. I discovered that Domenico was still constructing their marital bed in his workshop the night before, and instead of setting off on honeymoon, they sat chatting with friends late into the night, postponing their departure until the following day. None of us was surprised when they returned from the whole holiday just twenty-four hours later!

While we were in Italy, we took the opportunity to show my Mother, who had joined us, the sights, taking her to the Republic of San Marino to Florence and to Venice.

San Marino is about 25km from Rimini, the third smallest state in Europe (after the Holy See and Monaco) and claims to be the world's oldest republic. It was reportedly founded by a Christian stonemason called Maurinus in 301 AF and has around 28,000 inhabitants. My mother and I had visited the state some years before and our return visit reminded us of all that had happened in between.

Venice, of course, would not have been complete without a gondola ride. My Mother stepped aboard, wide–eyed and we drifted off into the labyrinth of canals that make up the cities streets. As we sat relaxing together, Barbara asked the gondolier whether Venice really *was* sinking and just how deep the water was. He commented that if the muck and debris on the canal bed was cleaned up, the water level might be a little lower! He was so engrossed in conversation that he didn't realise that he was coming to a crossroads and that another gondola was heading straight for us. 'Attento!' shouted Barbara, at which the gondolier swiftly stuck out his leg and bounced it against the building using his foot and the building in partnership as a brake. I wondered if the same trick would work in London rush hour traffic.

On the train to Florence we met Mary Lou, a young Australian girl who we bought lunch as we discovered that she hadn't eaten a proper meal for weeks. Mary Lou told us that she intended to visit England in July, so we invited her to stay with us when she arrived. When she learned that we were planning to go to Australia the following year and that Mark had a particular wish to see Sydney, she invited him to stay at her parent's home and said that they would be pleased to show him around the city. Both invitations were later fulfilled, establishing our friendship.

We arrived in Florence, saying goodbye to Mary Lou and began to explore the city.

Florence was as beautiful as ever, with its lengthening shadows to match lengthening queues outside the Uffizi, its wide piazza and an ice cream parlour on almost every corner.

We returned home to England and when my Mother came to stay with us for a fortnight soon afterwards we gave her a guided tour of London. There were no braking gondoliers or sun drenched piazza of course, but we could show her lengthy queues: as we drove past Buckingham Palace she was thrilled to see an orderly line of Garden Party guests in their hats and finery. Every colour of the rainbow was represented as hats and dresses fluttered in the breeze like carnival flags. We were amused by just how patiently they were waiting to be allowed into the Palace garden. We heard later that on her return to Cassano my mother had talked about the sight for weeks. She would have been so proud to know that David would one day be invited to join that prestigious queue!

Later that same summer, our niece Sandra visited from Australia and Marina from Italy, and we became willing tour guides once again. We took Sandra to Hampton Court Palace with its rich royal connections, stunning painted ceilings and heavy oak furniture. Sandra was so impressed by a four-poster bed – which she had never seen before – that she resolved to have one made in Australia ready for her forthcoming marriage. She was true to her word and spent the equivalent of three and a half thousand pounds on it! (Excluding the mattress).

Marina and Barbara particularly enjoyed each other's company and I never knew what they would get up to in my absence. At that time there was an express helicopter transfer between Gatwick and Heathrow airports, so in the middle of an ordinary morning, Barbara suddenly had one of her good ideas. She asked Marina if she had ever been on a helicopter. When Marina said she hadn't, Barbara suggested that they immediately drop what they were doing and set off for Heathrow for the airborne 'chopper' trip to Gatwick. Marina was so excited that when the pilot heard that Marina was on holiday from Italy he made sure they had the seats with the best view and generally treated Marina as a VIP. They returned from Gatwick by coach and when I arrived home from work, they were both giggling like schoolgirls, waiting to tell me of their impulsive mini-adventure! With so much fun to be had in a helicopter from Heathrow, it wasn't a surprise when Marina asked if she might join us on our planned trip to Australia with Mark, later in the year.

Anthony graduated from Exeter in August, with a degree in Mathematics and Physics and opted to take a gap year. He followed a month's TEFL course to enable

Outside Wallington (Surrey) Restaurant, March 1981 with Maria, Franco, Mamma, Enzo & Mario

Barlow Road, Hampton July 1984. Anthony give s Dad a lift on his birthday

Great Crosby Liverpool June 1983. Barbara, Mario and Barbara's sister Helen with Aunty Marjorie

Barlow Road, 1983. The Three Students - David, Anthony & Mark

Adelaide Jan. 1984. Sister Rosa's home with Mamma, Mario, Maria, Rosa and Brother Enzo

him to teach English as a foreign language and took a job at a school in Somma Lombardo in Italy. It came with a fully furnished flat and a small car. He knew no-one in Somma Lombardo on his arrival but he soon made friends. When Barbara and I visited him the following summer, we were invited to the homes of several of his students and given some insight into their fondness for our eldest son. One family owned a trattoria opposite Anthony's flat and the owner told us that he would have been quite happy for Anthony to have free meals every day, as it was so beneficial to his children to have the opportunity to make English conversation. Anthony had understandably declined this generous offer and continued to pay for his meals. Any incidental conversation came as an added extra – for both parties.

Our own Australian travel plans were shaping up nicely, and just after Christmas of 1983, the start date of our long awaited trip to Australia with Mark and Marina arrived.

Marina was unable to share our flight and had to follow the next day, but Mark, Barbara and I were upgraded to First Class, served champagne and offered the most fabulous meal, the result of which was my sleeping until our arrival in Bombay – eight hours later! Mark, meanwhile had been avidly listening, in 'is it true/isn't it?' mode, to a tale shared by a disabled man in his forties who was sitting alongside him. He 'confided' in Mark that he was carrying drugs in the inner-tubes of his wheelchair and that he was disembarking in Bombay where he would dispose of the drugs for a considerable profit. After a short break in Bombay – where the wheelchair smuggler did indeed apparently end his journey – we flew on to Adelaide.

In the arrivals hall in Adelaide at the end of our long journey we were overjoyed to see that my Mother was part of the welcoming party, although that joy turned to sadness when we later discovered the reason. We didn't realise at that moment that my sister Maria was seriously ill. She had expressed a wish to see my Mother and had arranged for her to fly out so that we could all be together as a family. Maria was suffering from bowel cancer and was admitted to hospital for treatment a few days later.

While we were in Adelaide, Marina, Barbara and I took a five day trip up the Murray River while Mark went to Sydney to meet up with Mary-Lou, as arranged the previous summer, en route to Florence. We visited the Barossa Valley, one of Australia's premier vineyard districts, where, even as an Italian I was impressed by the quality of the wine. During our stay we enjoyed both some not-so-Australian exploits: camel rides at Victor Harbour, and some very Ozzie sights: Kangaroo Island and the sight of Christmas decorations in summer. We also learned a lesson in self defence – that hats hung with corks are not just an eccentric fashion accessory, but an essential weapon in the battle against the numerous and persistent flies!

January heralded our return home, but when we said our goodbyes at the airport Maria clung to me in tears. She was reluctant to let me go, fearful that she might not see me again. The four of us returned sadly to London before Marina flew homeward to Italy.

Easter 1984 saw us weaving our way through the crowds into Salisbury Cathedral where we gathered to watch a special performance of The Passion of Christ. It was special because David was acting in the production with students from Cambridge, taking the part of Jesus. It was a poignant and very personal performance and so convincing that at the moment where Christ finally dies on the cross Barbara jumped with shock. Mark had to gently remind her that David was only acting.

Oxford, 2 Dec. 1984. Mark & David
on their 21st Birthday

The twins graduated from their respective universities in 1985 to follow very different paths:

David took a job as a research assistant for David Alton MP (now Lord Alton). Together they campaigned and raised funds for a Russian Christian man who had been imprisoned as a conscientious objector, successfully securing his release. Their shared Christian faith and political passion meant that 'The Two Davids' became firm friends.

Mark, meanwhile, headed for another continent. In June 1985, instead of remaining in England for his graduation ceremony, he travelled to North Africa, one of a group of forty students .They spent two months travelling through Morocco, Niger, Upper Volta and Algeria in two huge trucks.

Water was short and severely rationed, with only one cup allowed for washing. It was inevitable then, that the most fastidious of the young men would fall head-first into a cess-pit to the sympathetic amusement of the whole team.

When a group of Bedouins on camels passed by, the very different parties stopped to greet each other. Noticing some of the young ladies in Mark's party, the Bedouins offered to buy one of the girls for ten camels. To her extreme annoyance the boys momentarily agreed!

When later on the journey they stopped to cook a meal for their crowd of twenty a group of forty Africans turned up unexpectedly and their faith and resourcefulness was severely put to the test. As the rule of the desert is that one gives hospitality to travellers, they were obliged to share their meal. Although they had only prepared food for twenty, there was somehow enough for sixty – with extras for second helpings: a veritable modern day feeding of the five thousand!

On his return from Africa, Mark was thinner, somewhat grubby and carrying hardly any luggage as he had given most of his belongings away. But he had enjoyed a challenging and rewarding journey and looked happy and fulfilled.

Barbara and I continued our travels a little closer to home.

The Piano Tuners Association annual AGM and conference is held at venues all over the United Kingdom, and has often given us an opportunity to visit somewhere we've never been before – or to catch up with old friends.

On one occasion Barbara discovered the beautiful Cotswold village of Broadway, to which we have returned many times. On another we were able to visit 'Auntie Marjorie'.

During the war, Barbara and her sister Helen were evacuated to Crosby, near Liverpool to stay with a family which consisted of a Father and his daughter Marjorie, who Barbara and Helen came to know as 'Auntie Marjorie'. As the 1985 PTA conference was held at a hotel in Southport we invited Auntie Marjorie to join us for dinner on the last evening. On that occasion the Mayor of Southport was invited, and as Auntie Marjorie knew him (who, of note, didn't Auntie Marjorie know in the area?!) she was delighted to attend.

As we drove to Southport in anticipation, we reminded each other of a previous visit for Auntie Marjorie's 70th birthday party. Barbara's sister, Helen, had travelled with us and stayed with Auntie Marjorie in her flat, while Barbara and I had booked into a local hotel. As we only had an hour to get ready for Auntie Marjorie's special birthday dinner, we decided to share a bath together. On arriving back at the flat in more than good time Auntie Marjorie was pleased but amazed that we had managed to be so prompt. When we told her we had shared a bath in order to speed things up she looked shocked and stunned, but quickly recovered to remark, "Well, at least you are on time for dinner."

She was a rather eccentric character, very outspoken and given to more than honest remarks. Sometimes, in the middle of a sentence, she would make a sound like 'pip' to the great amusement of the boys who tried hard to stifle the giggling that followed. When Auntie Marjorie died in 1990 we found that she had pre-arranged the most lavish reception at The Blundell Sands Hotel in Crosby for all her friends and family to enjoy following her funeral. It was a perfectly, eccentrically, characteristic and wonderfully extravagant farewell.

In October 1985, we broadened our travel horizons once more with a trip to Portugal – including a day trip by coach to Seville. The coach set out very early in the morning and was supposed to arrive by lunchtime to long-promised paella. Unfortunately the coach was late, the paella had been eaten and the nearest alternative for most of the English coach-load was egg and chips in an 'Engleesh' Cafe. Barbara and I were horrified at such a compromise in such a place, and spent some time pounding the backstreets of Seville until we found what we were looking for: a typical Spanish restaurant full of Spaniards eating a late and lazy lunch. We enjoyed a fabulous feast of calamari and vegetables which fuelled us much more appropriately for the sightseeing that followed.

On another evening we visited a typical Portuguese village restaurant where a three piece band had assembled to entertain us. The band members looked rather dejected and subdued, completely devoid of enthusiasm or inspiration: their instruments as tarnished as they were. Eventually, I could stand it no longer and approached the band leader to ask if they would play 'O sole mio'. As they began, I hopped up next to them and burst into the words that I knew were more familiar words to our English coach party: 'Just one Cornetto!' I bellowed 'Give it to me!' This had an immediate and positive effect on the whole party – band included – who joined in heartily, and a jolly evening resulted.

On our final excursion, we visited Lisbon with its magnificent statue of Christ which echoes the elevated form in Rio de Janeiro. We toured the gilded St Anthony's Chapel in Lagos and walked on the very tip of the Portuguese peninsula with its vast panoramic view of the Atlantic.

As we travelled home, another holiday location was ticked off on our imaginary list.

In February 1986 it was David's turn to make headlines in the Campanale family news. He stood for election as a councilor in Hook ward, the Royal Borough of Kingston upon Thames, representing the Social Democrats, the SDP.

He quickly found that having an identical twin in Mark was a great asset during election campaigns, as his future constituents were amazed that David Campanale appeared to be 'everywhere at once'. He was probably the only politician who appeared to be able to kiss two babies, two miles apart at exactly the same time.

On May 8th Barbara made her signature special chocolate cake and we took a bottle of champagne to Kingston Guildhall to await the results of the count. We were equally prepared to eat the cake and drink the champagne whether to commiserate or celebrate, but when the results were declared, David had won. He had become the youngest councillor for his party in London at just 22, turning over a big Conservative majority. In our excitement we had forgotten to bring a knife to cut the cake, but a friendly policeman came to our rescue with his pen-knife and he and others joined in the celebration. He also turned a blind eye to David climbing onto the ancient stone where 7 Saxon Kings had been crowned, with mum's cake in one hand and champagne in the other.

David's work as a councillor often included visits to the Young Offenders unit at Feltham, where he always arrived typically casually dressed. During one visit a senior Labour councillor mistook him for an inmate and turned to him to ask "And why are you here?" David simply answered: "For exactly the same reason that you are!" It took a few moments for the penny to drop.

Four years later, David was re-elected, with a bigger share of the vote. Knowing how committed he was to his constituents – with and without his twin – we were not surprised.

In March 1986, with our Silver Wedding Anniversary approaching, I decided a special treat was in order. So I suggested to Barbara that we fly to New York by Concorde for a three day stay at the Waldorf Astoria followed by a voyage home on the QE II. I waited for the whoops of delight at the glamour and elegance of my offer. But Barbara, never one to choose luxury over adventure, said that she was not interested, and would prefer to go make for an entirely different destination – Iceland. She had once enjoyed a visit to her school friend Jennifer and family in Iceland and was keen for me to see the country too. So for our silver wedding celebrations we flew to Rejkjavik. I was amazed at the contrast between the barren snow covered landscape and the brightly lit city. Instead of the champagne of the Astoria, we enjoyed the complimentary champagne of our Rejkjavik hotel; in place of the Empire State building, we gazed at the Blue Lagoons and glaciers of Iceland. We had been married for twenty five years – yet to me the words 'Ciao Mario' from that beautiful girl in white seemed to have been spoken only a moment ago.

David's graduation from Oxford, which had been deferred for a year by choice, was held on a sunny June day in the hallowed literary surroundings of The Sheldonian Theatre. The ceremony – traditionally in Latin – was attended by the immediate family, all dressed in their finery. Following lunch in the University College Hall David took us punting on the river, bringing back memories of gondola rides in Venice. It was a Red Letter Day for all of us and Barbara and I shook hands, as is customary on such days, as a mark of parental achievement.

A month or two later, Mark flew out to Nairobi to work for four weeks for an environmental company who subsequently sponsored him to do a Postgraduate course in agricultural economics at Wye College in Kent. He also met Lotte, the girl he would later marry.

Anthony, meanwhile, had followed a postgraduate course in Computers and Artificial Intelligence and had, by this point, been working for Barclays Bank for a year. We were able to reflect on the joy of three special sons, of whom we were both immensely proud.

Barbara and I took our usual trip to Italy that summer, and on our journey back through France towards Macon, began looking for overnight accommodation, trying several small hotels without success. It was nine in the evening before we realised that the nearest large town where we might have more luck – the ominously named, Nevers – was twenty five miles way. We set out to reach it, but en route discovered a small hotel/restaurant by the roadside and went in to ask if we could be accommodated for the night. The owner told us, in French, that they were full up-and closed. But her daughter, working nearby, heard us speaking in English and asked us what it was we needed. She was rather more welcoming than her mother and explained that they did have one room. It was unfortunately lacking any kind of bathroom facilities, she said, but we were welcome to use it. Barbara, thinking of the practicalities, asked what we were to do in the event of needing the bathroom during the night.

The girl told us, almost in the style of an adventure story: we were to go out through the outside door in the corridor close to our room, walk down the steep external staircase, cross the courtyard towards the front of the hotel – which, by the way, was on the main road and slip through the main entrance to use the hotel facilities. Barbara, filled with visions of a nocturnal trek in her nightdress, said that we couldn't possibly do such a thing in the middle of the night. As a last resort, she asked, in a mixture of French and Italian, "Madame, avez vous un chamber pot damettr sot u lit?" The girl went off to ask her mother for this refined receptacle and came back with the reply-in perfect English: "You can have a bucket." Barbara's face was a picture.

There was, in fact, at least a washbasin in the room, but the whole episode became hilarious. Once we agreed to take the room – and pay for it (bucket included) the mother's attitude improved no end and she offered us dinner and drinks: for some reason we didn't have too many.

As we got to know the daughter – Martine – we discovered that she was keen to learn English and improve her language skills by visiting England. We offered to help in any way we could, and since that first adventurous introduction, we have tried to call in whenever we are passing. Sometimes we have even stayed overnight.

The following March was a sad time for us. We heard of the deaths of my Mother's sister Faustina in Cassano, and my sister Maria, in Australia.

Maria had been well for two years following the treatment she had undergone while we were visiting her, but she died aged 44, leaving a husband and three children.

Barbara also attended the funeral of her friend Jennifer, in Exeter. She had many happy memories of her school friend, one of which I shared.

Barbara had gone to visit Jennifer and her family while they were living in Iceland and while she was there I needed to telephone her. Not knowing Jennifer's number, I telephoned International Directory Enquiries and was asked for the country I needed to call: 'Iceland' I replied. The operator then asked me for Jennifer's surname, to which I replied, seriously and correctly; 'Freeze'. The operator with some annoyance and impatience told me 'This is no time for jokes!' It took me some time to convince him that Jennifer's surname really *was* Freeze.

In April we felt in need of a recuperative break and decided to go to Italy for three weeks, traveling through Calabria en route to Sicily. We stopped at Taormina where a lavatory visit was necessary and promptly found ourselves on another of our Bathroom Adventures!

Having been charged an exorbitant 200 Lire for a visit to the lavatory, I refused the attendant's offer of toilet paper, wondering how much I might be charged for such a luxury. However, a return visit later in the day made that luxury a necessity, and I was somewhat taken aback when I was given an accurate and deliberate count of just seven small pieces of paper. I asked for more, but was refused. While sparingly rationing myself in a cubicle, the more senior of the two female attendants began shouting and kicking its door in fury at my request for more paper. On emerging from the toilet, having succeeded in my seven piece challenge, I felt more than inclined to kick and shout back in retaliation. But remembering that we were in Sicily and wondering about the attendant's family connections – I restrained myself!

Hospitality of any kind was obviously not a widespread local gift. That night, on

June 1984. Hampton Hill.
Mario & Barbara

University College, Oxford June 1986. David's Graduation
Day with the proud parents & brothers Anthony & Mark

our way to Agrigento we stayed overnight in a small hotel, and when we went down to breakfast the following morning found that none of the tables in the dining room had been cleared from the previous night. When the staff needed to send out for bread and kept us waiting for some considerable time, serving only lukewarm tea, I was outraged. I demanded they gave us our bill and documents so that we could leave. They were not at all apologetic as it appeared that this slovenly behaviour was quite acceptable to the locals. Thankfully a nearby bar did not share the same standards of hospitality and served us delicious brioche and cappuccino – on clean tables.

Our drive through Sicily was a beautiful one. Spring flowers and heady red poppies filled the surrounding countryside. We arrived at Agrigento, where the surrounding vegetation blends fittingly with the ochre and brown of the Doric Temples which attract thousands of tourists. It was these temples that we headed for. Despite the Grecian splendour of our surroundings, there were, naturally (in more ways than one) the inevitable problems with lavatories. Everyone tended to head for the local bar, where there was only one toilet with a broken light-fitting which stubbornly refused to shed light on anyone's proceedings. Consequently it was in a disgusting state. When I complained to the proprietor, saying that I was surprised that better facilities had not been provided in such a popular tourist area, he was sympathetic. He explained that the local authorities had built a toilet block at the rear of his bar, but that they couldn't find anyone to work as an attendant. There was also the problem of a local water supply – there simply wasn't any.

As we left (legs crossed) we decided to pay a surprise visit to my cousin who lived in the spa town of Sciacca – at least they had lavatories and water.

Sciacca sits at the foot of the Cattabellotta hills with a 'balcony' over the sea, the Piazza Scandaliato. It is here that the townspeople gather, especially for parties, festivals and carnivals, for which the townspeople have a passion.

I only had the address of my aunt, the widow of my mother's eldest brother – but was confident that I could find their house. When we arrived, neighbours told us that my Aunt was now living in a retirement home, but that they were able to give us the address of my two cousins.

After a little searching along narrow streets dappled with sun, we found my cousin Peppino and were given a tremendous welcome. Within half an hour the other members of the family started arriving to welcome us, many of them with food and wine tucked under their arms – it was obviously party time – and we were honoured guests. It was all wonderfully overwhelming.

We sat down to eat and drink together and during the more reflective moments of conversation, I explained to my cousin's wife that Barbara had benefited from brain surgery and asked her to make allowances for her as she often became tired. The family was especially sympathetic and explained that they quite understood. Their son had died in his twenties while undergoing an examination at a Rome hospital to investigate symptoms of what was found to be a brain tumour. They were amazed to hear about Barbara's operation, performed so much earlier in 1966, and to see how relatively well she was. Barbara and I felt newly grateful for her recovery and for the opportunity to be sitting in Italy surrounded by family some twenty years later.

We were made so welcome by so many cousins and given such a feast – a table laden with delicious food which mysteriously appeared – that I couldn't help feeling that we were being more than compensated for our earlier inhospitable experiences! (Even the toilet arrangements were more than adequate).

We were sad to leave such a warm and happy family scene, but our holiday time was running out and we had to make for home, refreshed and rejuvenated. As we did, so we reflected on all we had seen and heard and talked about and reminded ourselves to make the most of the precious gift of time – and life – that we had been given.

Faenza Italy, January 1986. Mario & Anna Casamassima's home in celebration for our visit and for a new year. Anna joining Mario with an Italian song

The Rhoda Macgrows Theatre Woking, Surrey July 1984. On the back stage stairs Mario with dancers in a Russian tap dancing display

CHAPTER NINE

A song for you and me

Barbara had continued with regular appointments at The Royal Marsden and the National Hospital for Neurology, but in the summer of 1987, began to feel depressed. Anti-depressants appeared to have little effect causing us some concern as to the origin of the depression.

But in July we heard the good news that Mark had passed his postgraduate exams in Agricultural Economics at Wye College and Barbara was kept busy with visiting friends from Italy, Chile and the USA and arranged and enjoyed a school reunion for her friends from Oxted County Grammar School. All of this busy-ness helped her stay as positive as possible.

We continued our worldwide travels in August with another trip to Boston, where we were met once more by my cousin Geno, this time staying at his brother Frank's house in Watertown.

Another Boston cousin, Franco, invited us to lunch at his home and asked us if we liked rabbit, chicken and lobster. We assumed that he was to make a choice between the three for our forthcoming meal. But we sat down at the table to be served with anti-pasti, followed by mounds of spaghetti, then rabbit, chicken *and* lobster in turn! The food was marvelous – if a challenge – and was equally enjoyed by all of us, especially Geno's 87 year old mother who tackled the food – especially the lobster – with great gusto. Who says appetite diminishes with age?

Later in our stay, after yet another sumptuous lunch, Geno took us to an Armenian restaurant for dinner. The food was delicious, but the portions so generous that we wished we had eaten much less at lunchtime in order to have the appetite to do it justice. The highlight of the evening, however, was not on a plate but on the dance floor: a belly dancer in chiffon and veils sat on all the gentlemen's knees, encouraging them to tuck a few dollars into her bra. I could hardly refuse such an invitation! At the end of the evening, everyone linked arms to join in an Armenian dance, circulating around the restaurant.

We were keen to visit the Niagara Falls while we were in the States, so we flew from Boston to Niagara, but on arrival were at a loss as to how to find the hotel we had booked.

I heard a woman nearby speaking Italian and attracted by my native tongue, asked if she might be able to help us. She was charming and friendly, and we discovered that she was working as a tour guide offering commentaries to Italian speaking tourists. She was keen to help us and said that her boss, an Irish tour guide called Jimmy, was about to arrive and she was sure he would help us further. Jimmy more than helped. He took us to our hotel, arranged lunch for us at The Minolta Tower

Restaurant and booked us onto a boat trip which crossed beneath the thundering water. Barbara and I couldn't believe our luck at having met such a friendly pair. Jimmy was so willing to organise everything for us with the minimum of fuss, even though it was his 'day job'!

In December it was Anthony's turn for adventure and he set off on a tran-Siberian tour from Moscow to Tashkent. As he knew it would be bitterly cold he equipped himself with a pair of high German leather boots, an ankle length coat, a wide belt and a fur hat. He looked exactly like a Russian soldier and was advised not to wear the whole outfit together in case he was mistaken for a Russian military deserter and arrested.

His trip was a great success and he returned with a small but odd assortment of gifts: some Russian china teacups and three fur hats as there had been so little to buy. His currency? Jeans: a rare and much prized fashion statement as far as the Russians were concerned.

Just before Christmas, David invited me to entertain the residents at a retirement home in his Hook constituency, by playing the guitar and singing. Barbara made well over a hundred mince pies for the occasion and we duly arrived to share in the Christmas celebrations. Before I sang, I helped out by serving sherry to the residents. As I did, so one old lady asked when my father was going to sing, obviously mistaking me for David. I had to explain that I was, in fact, 'the father.' To complicate matters further, once I did start singing another resident told Barbara that she thought her 'son' sang very well, while a third commented that the mince pies were 'okay', but that she preferred puff pastry. Barbara seemed to survive the evening's doubts about her age and culinary skills remarkably well!

Mark meanwhile, remained in Tanzania in Moshi Town, near the Kilimanjaro Mountains. He was supervising the export of various foodstuffs, including coffee and papaya for a Swiss company.

He had great sympathy for those he worked with, especially the Tanzanian farm workers. Mark, who had gained a Masters degree in Agricultural Economics at Wye

Watertown, Mass. USA August 1987. Barbara & cousin Frank's wife Sandy having Gelato Delizioso!

Boston USA August 1987. Zia Caterina & Geno eating with gusto the third course of Lobster

College the previous year, enjoyed the physical work at the animal feed factory. He often travelled out to the farms by truck to pick up ingredients and worked alongside the others mixing up feed by spade and selling the bags to the visiting farmers.

While in Kilimanjaro, Mark was allocated a bungalow and the help of a local man called Onessimo who was his cook and housekeeper. He was also given a bodyguard called Lazarus who was a Masai warrior. Lazarus, however, did not always demonstrate the behaviour or know the fortune of a true warrior.

On one occasion there was a disturbance outside the bungalow involving armed men and poor Lazarus, armed only with a bow and arrow, fled and hid in the bushes. Fortunately the incident ended peacefully and Lazarus' rather basic weaponry was not put to the test.

In another incident, the farm lorry, loaded with produce ready to go to market, trapped Lazarus against a wall causing extensive and serious injuries to his chest and stomach. After gently positioning him on top of the boxes, the lorry set off to the local hospital with Mark following behind in his pick-up truck. Because the roads were so rough and the lorry driver was driving as fast as possible in order to get Lazarus to the hospital, disaster struck and the lorry's crankshaft broke. Poor Lazarus was the victim of a second accident in as many hours and had to be painfully moved once more; from the lorry to the back of Mark's truck. At the hospital, Mark was told that Lazarus urgently needed a blood transfusion, but as the hospital didn't keep a supply of blood they had to recycle Lazarus's own. Amazingly, after one or two setbacks, Lazarus survived-somewhat living up to his name.

Africa was not without its risks for Mark, and in February 1988 we received a call from Tanzania to say that Mark had developed symptoms of suspected appendicitis. Fortunately he was being looked after by an English nurse, as the clinical care at the Kilimanjaro hospital was very poor. As post-operative care there would be inadequate, he was advised to wait for a few days before deciding whether to have an operation. Together with Mark's girlfriend, Lotte, we managed to persuade him to return home so that he could be examined at Kingston hospital where any surgery needed could be performed with greater safety. The arrangements to bring Mark home required over thirty telephone calls between England and Tanzania. Curiously, during that time, David – his twin – also felt unwell.

Mark arrived at Heathrow a few days later and we took him straight to Kingston hospital where he underwent a thorough examination.

Extensive and specialist tests by the medical team discovered that the pain had been caused by a viral infection resulting from water-snail disease, which is common in Africa, and that surgery was not needed for appendicitis.

Mark was directed to the Institute of Tropical Diseases in London who prescribed a course of treatment which eliminated the infection. We couldn't help wondering what would have happened if Mark had taken the risk of unnecessary surgery in Tanzania. Although Mark was keen to return to Africa we persuaded him to remain in England once the treatment had finished, so that he could make a full recovery.

Around this time, Barbara began to notice that she was finding it difficult to hear people when they were speaking, so we arranged a hearing test at St George's Hospital in London. A thorough hearing assessment confirmed that the hearing in her right ear was diminishing. A trip to see Mike Yarwood, the impersonator, at the Fairfield Halls in Croydon, less conventionally confirmed that all was not well, as Barbara had great difficulty in hearing him, despite considerable professional amplification.

At the beginning of May, a routine scan at The Royal Marsden did little to encourage us. We already knew that there was little that could be done to halt Barbara's likely deterioration – we simply had to continue to 'live for the day'.

So at the end of May, Barbara and I went to Italy for two weeks and were introduced by my mother to the Lofiase family, whose daughter, Isa, wished to visit England to practice her English.

In early August Isa and her friend Anna-Maria arrived in London to stay with us for two weeks. Anna-Maria was more confident in her English than Isa, but they still chatted to each other in Italian whenever they got the chance!

We took the girls to Devon to stay with our friends Marjorie and John; to Oxford and to Stratford-Upon-Avon, where we enjoyed their delight in the historic surroundings.

One evening we gave a dinner party including the two girls, David's Hungarian friend Zsolt and his mother, and two of my customers. As I looked around the table I realised that we were a party of three Italians, two Hungarians, one German and three English people: hardly the best company for Isa as she tried to improve her English! When Isa and Anna-Maria left for home a few days later, I lightheartedly suggested to Isa that when she returned it might be better if she did so alone, without a chattering Italian girlfriend, her opportunities to speak English might then improve!

At the end of September, Barbara, Anthony and I returned to Adelaide for the wedding of my niece Sandra (whose marital bed had been inspired by the four posters at Hampton Court) to Toni. We 'stopped over' in Perth, where Anthony had arranged to spend a few days with friends. He intended to join us in Adelaide later – after traveling from Perth to Adelaide by Greyhound Bus, a journey of some twenty four hours.

The wedding, in the local Catholic church had more than it's fair share of beauty in the bride and attendants. As is the custom, everyone returned to their own homes after the ceremony, meeting up in the evening for a reception that went on until the small hours. The following day there was a big gathering in a marquee at my sister's home.

On the way home from Adelaide we stopped in Sydney to stay with our friend, Bob – with whom I had worked on that special piano assignment many years before – and his wife, Anna. While in a shopping mall in the city, we were somewhat bemused to see Geoffrey Archer signing his novels in a bookshop.

It made us question whether we really were in Australia!

We met up with Anthony, who had returned to visit his friends in Sydney, and who was now sporting a large scratch on his leg, caused, he claimed – to our alarm – by a shark.

Barbara and I explored Sydney on our own enjoying the double-decker trains with shopping malls at each station; the variety of eateries and the beautiful Queen Victoria Building. We spent the evening with Ignazio, an old school friend from Cassano, and his wife, in their beautiful home.

On our return to England, some friends of David rather unexpectedly came to stay. They were young politicians active in the emerging opposition in communist Hungary, who, because of a misunderstanding, had not been met by a member of the Foreign Office and were left without accommodation.

We were rather amused at becoming unofficial government hosts, but were more than delighted to offer them hospitality in our home.

In November, David went to Hungary on a return visit to appear on Hungarian television to speak about democracy. Having met his friends, we felt sure that his own welcome party would not have been forgotten in Hungary.

In March 1989 Barbara and I – this time with our friend Glenys – set off for Italy once more. We arrived in Caen and then made a detour to visit the beautiful Chartres Cathedral before heading for Digoin. En route we visited our 'night time trek' friend Martine and her family and enjoyed a Boeuf Bourguignonne at their restaurant. It was the most magnificent dish: rich, warming and absolutely delicious. Its wonderfully authentic French flavour lives in my taste bud memory to this day.

We reached the Aosta Valley in Northern Italy by the evening, driving through sloping valleys of breathtaking scenery. The Aosta Valley is a mountainous Alpine region in North West Italy, bordered by France to the West, Switzerland to the North and the Piedmont region to the South and West. It was here that we found accommodation in a very pleasant hotel.

While eating dinner in a nearby restaurant we noticed that an English language class was going on nearby and couldn't resist introducing ourselves. When we discovered that the group was discussing Pavarotti, Barbara knew she had just the thing to help the conversation along. She opened her bag, rummaged around for a while and pulled out the photograph that had been taken of our family with Pavarotti at The Royal Opera House several years earlier. The group was delighted at Barbara's instant and very personal visual aid.

The following morning we set off in heavy rain and after struggling with driving and visibility for many miles, I phoned Marina in Rimini on impulse and asked if she had room where we might stay for the night. She welcomed us with a hearty supper and we were able to continue our journey to Assisi the following day under clear skies.

Assisi has attracted visitors and pilgrims from all over the world for nearly 800 years. It is filled with churches and dominated, ironically, by the unpretentious figure and personality of St Francis. The hills around the town offer spectacular views over the surrounding countryside, its large Fortress, Rocca Maggiore, towers over the town as if to protect its spiritual heritage.

We stayed high in the hills above the town at The Country House Hotel and learnt that the following evening there was to be a procession from St Clare's church down to St Francis's Basilica. We decide that this was an event not to be missed.

It was a clear but bitterly cold evening, so we wrapped up warm and made our way down to the town to wait with the slowly gathering crowds for the procession to begin. We watched fascinated as one by one, first the shop lights, and then the street lights were extinguished. Flares and candles were put in sconces on the walls and the crowd grew strangely and reverently silent. Eventually, we heard chanting which came ever closer and then the rumbling sound of heavy drum beats as the procession came into view in the gathering   dusk. The drummers were at the head of the procession followed by the Brothers from the church. Although they walked together as a group, the Brothers appeared to be lost in their solitude and reflection. They wore long shapeless robes and their heads were bowed in pointed hoods with mere slits through which to see the path they should follow. They wore chains around their ankles which clunked heavily and dragged as they walked, their ankles were chaffed and their bare feet looked blue with cold. Every so often the group would stop to chant prayers and then move along on their way while the watching crowd stood in silent awe. The whole procession took about two hours to pass by in great solemnity. But once it had disappeared completely from view, the roadside crowd dispersed in chattering clumps and rushed into the contrasting colour and conviviality of local restaurants and pizzerias to warm up with hot food and wine. We shared a delicious pizza which was prepared in front of us, the smell of dough and hot toppings wafting into the night air, sharpening our appetites.

I couldn't help wondering what the brothers would be eating for their supper – or if they would eat anything at all.

Our meals in Italy were often a source of amusement, courtesy of the menu.

On the following Monday we found that the menu at our favourite restaurant was written in three languages and proclaimed, in English, that 'Parma Jam and Melon' were being served. We called over the Grandmother in charge of this family–run establishment and explained to her what 'jam' meant. She was rather perturbed and said that she would correct her Granddaughter who had written the menu. We asked, then, if perhaps we might just have the melon. To which she replied: 'Are you Italian? Surely you know that it is not the season for melon!' By this time we – and most of the rest of the restaurant guests -were in hysterics.

The next morning, to our delight, the temperature had risen by several degrees and we were able to sit in the square drinking coffee and enjoying the spring sunshine. Sadly, there was still no Parma jam – or melon – available.

The following Saturday was our wedding anniversary, so Barbara and I particularly wanted to find a special restaurant for a special meal. But all the hotels and restaurants were fully booked and in the end we spotted – or rather sniffed out – a kiosk

in the square which had roasted pork with herbs and spices on a spit roast overnight. The smell was tantalizing. We approached the stall and watched as the meat was carved into succulent slices. We bought some, wrapped it up to keep it warm and carried it back to our hotel with the intention of eating it in our room. When we arrived, we felt rather too much like smugglers for our consciences to bear. So I told the owner our story, asking her permission to eat in the hotel bedroom, rather than do so surreptitiously in guilt! She said that she would lay the table in the main room so that we could eat there, as long as we finished by 9pm so that the other guests wouldn't find out and expect the same concessions. So, there we sat, celebrating our wedding anniversary with almost smuggled pork on an almost forbidden table and against the clock!

Having overcome a few car problems and an alternator repair in Perugia, we continued on to the beautiful and historic town of Siena.

The year 1348 was a memorable one for Siena – for all the wrong reasons. More than two-thirds of the prosperous population was killed by The Black Death, halting the town's rapid economic progression but leaving behind a perfect example of a medieval town. Siena is a treasure trove of tiny streets and alleyways in which it is easy – even advisable – to lose yourself. At the heart of the town is the Campo, a stunning heart shaped Piazza fringed by cafes, the perfect place to sit with a coffee or a glass of wine and watch the world go by.

We enjoyed the Duomo and sought out some sticky Panforte of Siena: hard nougat containing whole almonds. And I couldn't resist withdrawing some money from Europe's oldest 13th century bank.

After Siena we headed for the heat and chaotic bustle of Rome and The Lancelot Hotel, one of our favourite places to stay. The hotel is run along English lines with fruit and flowers everywhere. Guests are encouraged to sit at communal tables to eat in order to get to know one another, so it is inevitable that various international friendships are easily made as a result of the sharing of coffee, fruit and brioche.

Glenys had long wanted to visit Rome and kept pinching herself to check that she really was there at last.

The following day we visited St Peter's Basilica and the Sistine chapel where we craned our necks willingly to wonder at Michelangelo's breathtaking paintings which cover every inch of the expansive ceilings. We marvelled at the idea of this tiny man: artist, sculptor, architect and poet, busily painting for most of his lifetime with his team of assistants, checking every hand and foot and cloud that was painted for flaws and inaccuracies. We chuckled at the idea that so much of it was done in competition with fellow artist Raphael, whose charm and sophistication outdid Buonarroti's apparent lack of social graces, but could not outshine his brilliant artistry.

Moving from culture to comedy, as so befits Italy, we returned to the hotel to hear about the adventures of a group of American tourists: one woman had lost her husband in the crowd, and becoming rather anxious, she approached a group of carabinieri to explain what had happened. "Can you help me?" She asked in some distress, "I have lost my husband." To which one of them replied: "Don't worry Madam, there are five of us – which one would you like?"

We couldn't be sure, but the three of us rather thought she wished she had taken them up on the offer!

Acquaviva was our destination the following morning where we had arranged to lodge with Signora Cafaro, as we'd done so many times before.

Glenys's room was sandwiched between Sig.ra Cafaro's bedroom and a very loud refrigerator which clicked itself on and off every fifteen minutes. Poor Sig.ra Cafaro's coughing and nocturnal pacing added to the night-time noise resulting in a very disturbed night for poor Glenys. We had to do something. So using the nearby Lofiase family as both an excuse and a refuge – "They will so benefit from speaking English with Glenys" – we arranged for her to have alternative accommodation with Isa and her family. Even there the notoriously unreliable and inappropriately named Acquaviva water supply let Glenys down: there was no running water in her bathroom!

We remained in Acquaviva for the remainder of our holiday visiting the pretty whitewashed villages of Alberello, Ostuni and Selva di Fasano and helped Glenys to soak up the sights, sounds and flavours of Southern Italy.

Glenys boarded the plane home at Bari airport with tears in her eyes and warm goodbyes from the Lofiase family ringing in her ears. The girls had adopted her as their Aunt – Zia Glenys – and made her first visit to Italy as memorable as it could possibly be.

In June, David travelled to the USA for the American Independence Day celebra-

tions and to visit to my cousin Geno, not knowing that he was about to become embroiled in an adventure worthy of a Le Carre novel.

In the middle of his visit he was called home at the invitation of ITN, and asked to go to Romania to help with making a secret report on the activities of President Ceausescu.

David travelled straight to Eastern Europe, knowing that his assignment was potentially a very dangerous one. He had been asked to film the destruction of village communities which had become widespread as a result of the Romanian government's policy of housing people in high rise flats.

When David arrived in Bucharest he was planning to meet up with fellow journalist Sue Lloyd-Roberts, but she failed to appear at their rendezvous. Neither did she turn up at his hotel. So, rather concerned, he sat in his hire car in the street and prayed about the situation. There was a sudden bang on the car window and someone from the hotel told him that there was a telephone call for him. It was Sue Lloyd-Roberts. She and her colleague had been arrested in Yugoslavia; David would have to manage on his own. The news did nothing to alleviate David's sense of danger, but certainly underlined the importance of his assignment.

He stayed one night, as anonymously as possible, in a ski resort and then spent the next couple of days filming. As he was on his own and vulnerable, he drove mainly on minor roads, constantly checking his car mirror in case he was being followed.

One evening, while he was taking a bath at the hotel he was told by the hotel management that he must move rooms. As the new hotel room had numerous mirrors on the walls, David was convinced that the room was bugged and that he was under surveillance: not a situation in which to get a good night's sleep!

Arrangements had been secretly made for David to meet Sue Lloyd-Roberts' uncle at an appointed place so that he could carry David's film – all on cassette tape

– safely home to ITN. He was told that Sue's uncle would be reading *The Times*: David was told to talk to him about cricket. The conversation over, David followed his new friend into the gentleman's toilet at a distance and gave him the tapes, keeping some less important tapes for himself in case there was a need for a decoy.

When David went to catch his plane home from Bucharest airport he was detained by officials who demanded that he handed over the tapes. He gave them the decoys – some innocuous tapes of scenery and children playing in a garden – which they destroyed in front of him without checking their content. He was then allowed to board the plane.

Meanwhile, Sue's ingenious uncle had a Sony walkman on which he pretended to listen to what appeared to be audio tapes on the flight home, tapping his feet and nodding his chin to their apparent rhythm. They were, of course, David's damning 'records' of Ceausescu's regime.

The following day the tapes were shown on television and David was interviewed by Tim Ewart on *The One O'Clock News*. As he was still a borough councillor, the local newspapers were full of Councillor David Campanale's exciting Romanian adventures.

David would continue his Eastern European travels the following October. This time with a rather less taxing trip to Hungary, reporting on the progress of Hungary's new democracy.

The month of July always sees a happy collision of birthdays in the Campanale family: mine on the 8th; my mother's on the 9th and Anthony's on the 11th. As my mother was staying with us that summer we decided to throw a party to celebrate all three family birthdays. So invitations were sent out to friends, family and neighbours and on the 9th July we prepared to celebrate, Campanale style!

Franco brought his band and set up on the patio as friends and family began to arrive. There was far too much food, copious amounts of wine, and laughter and conversation that drifted on into the long night. A lively time was had by all, even if – as one neighbour again suggested – our parties always remind him of the wedding scene from *The Godfather*.

What would the next year bring? We wondered.

Not content with the Campanale family's recent mix of intrigue and supposed notoriety, Barbara and I were planning yet another adventure of our own.

CHAPTER TEN:
Mario's Theme

Barbara and I had long wished to visit our cousins in Argentina, so we made plans to take a trip in November: the beginning of the Argentinian summer.

As we were travelling soon after the end of the Falklands War, there were no direct flights from London to Buenos Aires, but we secured a booking with a Brazilian airline which offered a stop over in Rio de Janeiro – somewhere we had always wanted to visit.

We checked into the Trocadero Hotel on Copacabana beach for two days, and began our tour of the city the following morning.

We travelled up the hillside by special train to take a close look at the forty metre high statue of Christ which stands high above the city overlooking the sea. We had, of course, witnessed its replica in Lisbon while on holiday in Portugal.

Afterwards we were taken by cable car to Sugarloaf Mountain and were told by the guide that we were passengers in a brand new Italian cable car which had recently replaced the previous German model: I found this very reassuring.

The views from the summit were breathtaking.

After lunch we were taken on an afternoon tour of the city itself. The contrasts we witnessed could not have been more striking: we passed the most luxurious of residences and the poorest of shanty dwellings, finally passing through the *Avenida* where the carnival takes place.

The following day we flew to Buenos Aires, enjoying upgrade Club Class seats and were met at Buenos Aires airport by my cousin Vincenzo and his brother–in –law, Michele, the husband of my cousin Marialucia.

Our journey to their home town of Tandil, 350km away, took over four hours, but we were warmly welcomed by my cousin Marialucia and told that we would be staying with her family.

We were immediately struck by the fact that their standard of living was basic despite their hard work. Michele was a barber spending half his day in a little shop attached to the house and the other half at the nearby military airbase, where he was employed cutting the hair of Argentinean air force officers. Marialucia sold cosmetics in the surrounding area as well as running a grocery shop at the front of the house. Their son Nicola worked in the local bank earning 90 dollars a month, which they considered to be a good salary. Everything that was imported was expensive and once again we noted that, as in Rio, alcohol was advertised to fuel cars instead of petrol.

The pavements in the town were uneven and irregular making them difficult to negotiate. We mentioned this 'up, down, watch your step' experience and were told that pavement repairs were the responsibility of home owners who often couldn't afford the work needed to maintain them.

At the same time we were amused to discover that to advertise a car for sale privately it was the custom to park the vehicle by the kerb side with an oil can on the roof!

The town, and the cars, seemed very outdated. But the ice-cream parlours – even to an Italian – were second to none. The local specialities included an ice-cream dipped in chocolate: *Helado Bagnada*. Of course we had to try them: they were delicious.

To welcome us, Marialucia arranged an indoor barbecue on a large grill over a metre long, onto which a large carcass of beef was lowered. As each part was ready to eat it was carved off and passed around: the smell of roast meat and charcoal was intoxicating.

Meat was cheap and plentiful, and large parties were often held outside when everyone brought their own knife to cut off the slices of delicious roast beef. The meat was washed down with a traditional herbal tea: *mate* which was served hot.

Although both Barbara and I did all we could to avoid eating or drinking anything which might cause us stomach problems, we did feel ill on one occasion so my cousin rang the doctor. As he also happened to be a friend, he was invited, with his wife, to stay for supper. It was only once the Pizza had been eaten and enjoyed that the doctor-also called Mario-turned his attention to his patients. He simply asked Michele for a spoon and used it to examine our tongues! We were amazed that he didn't carry any instruments but simply relied on what he had to hand.

We couldn't help noticing that the women worked hard for their families, but not always with due appreciation. One evening, when Michele had served us all with a drink, Marialucia was still busy preparing the evening meal. Barbara asked when she was going to sit down. Michele's immediate reply was "I don't know! Her place is in the kitchen!"

I commented to Nicola's wife Mirtha that she was an excellent housewife and mother, using the word '*brava*' which in Italian is complimentary. I was somewhat surprised when she walked away from me silently, and then discovered from her husband that I had referred to her as a woman of the streets! He must have explained the confusion, because she didn't appear to hold my comments against me.

When we left, Mirtha presented Barbara with a beautiful pair of scissors as a present. They had cost almost a third of her weekly wage.

We returned home at the beginning of December having been touched by the warmth and hospitality shown to us on our Argentinian trip.

In March 1990, Barbara and I went to the beautiful Georgian city of Bath to celebrate our wedding anniversary, it was our first visit. We were delighted with the golden stonework and the elegant architecture and took tea – with milk – in the Pump Rooms, to the accompaniment of musicians.

The following month, David's friend Kati, from Transylvania, came to visit. David met Kati, a journalist and photographer, on his travels in Hungary and Romania. She very much wanted to visit England because of David's position as a councillor. During her stay we took her to Marks and Spencer where she fell in love with the beautiful nightdresses on display, believing them to be wedding dresses. She then noticed a pair of pyjamas with rabbits appliquéd on the ankle. When I offered to buy them for her – they were way beyond the affordable bounds of her small salary – she almost jumped for joy and couldn't wait to get home to try them on!

In the local government elections on the 3rd of May David was re-elected as councillor for Hook ward and Barbara once again made her very large signature chocolate cake with which to celebrate. Sadly, our friendly and obliging policeman with his handy cake-cutting pen knife was nowhere to be seen.

In July, Rosa and Saverio arrived from Australia followed by my Aunt Marietta from the USA and we all travelled to Italy together for a holiday. We had all grown up together on the same street in Cassano, so our arrival in time for the Festa reminded us of happy times in days gone by.

Zia Marietta decided to treat several members of the family to a meal at a hillside restaurant, but the guest numbers somehow rose to twelve and when the bill arrived, poor Zia. Marietta found that she had wildly underestimated the cost: we were all asked to make up the shortfall, to much amusement all round!

We then visited Giovanna and Carlo, friends of Rosa and Saverio, who had returned to Italy from Australia to live in the hills above Termoli. When I asked Giovanna what she missed most about Australia her reply was immediate and surprising: "The gravy!"

Giovanna's brother lived in a monastery nearby and invited us to his birthday celebrations. We were honoured to be asked, but expected a somewhat frugal affair. So we were stunned to be faced with a table groaning with food, barrels of excellent wine and a scene resembling a medieval banquet.

Marietta returned to the USA from Italy, while Rosa and Saverio travelled to England to stay with us for six weeks. Before they left for home they threw a 'Farewell and Thankyou' barbecue at home for the family.

In the autumn Barbara and I visited Scotland, staying in a hotel on the banks of Loch Lomond, it was to be the first of many visits across the border.

We celebrated our 30th wedding anniversary the following March after which I travelled to Italy alone to visit my mother. David stayed with Barbara while I was away and on my return I was delighted to discover that he had filed all my photographs in albums in chronological order, giving shape to over thirty years of family life, travels, visits and entertaining friends.

The following summer marked our first visit to Ireland, paid for by Barbara's 'Auntie Marjorie'. We stayed in a little fishing village to the East of Dublin and in the evening called in at the Abbey Tavern.

It was full of tourists drinking Guinness and enjoying the entertainment provided by an eight piece band and Irish dancers. We found the atmosphere so lively that we resolved to make a return visit before the end of our holiday.

The following day we spent in Dublin visiting Trinity College and discovering the Book of Kells: an eighth century manuscript of the Gospels and the oldest book in Ireland.

We moved on to County Wicklow and south to Rosslaire where we found the Ferrycarrig Hotel with rooms overlooking the estuary. We thought it would suit us well and went inside to enquire about prices and vacancies. Unfortunately the prices matched the view – both were breathtaking! We declined the accommodation offer we were made and were about to leave discreetly when the manager appeared. He offered us an excellent suite of rooms at a reduced price simply, it seemed, because he had heard Barbara and I conversing in Italian. He said he had just returned from Italy where he had watched a world cup match and knew 'a little of the language' himself.

After two nights at the Ferrycarrig we travelled west – at the manager's sugges-tion – to 'see the best of Ireland.' En route we stopped at Waterford to visit the glass crystal factory, and then drove on to Cork, via Tipperary to the Muckross Hotel, in Killarny, which the Ferrycarrig manager had recommended. We discovered that the cost of the rooms was even higher than Ferrycarrig.

Once again we declined the offer of a room and turned to leave. As we started towards the door, the manager came downstairs and asked if he could help us. We told him that the manager of the Ferrycarrig had recommended the hotel, but that the prices were far more than we were able to afford. He quickly said that as the hotel had recently been refurbished he was prepared to reduce the price by nearly half, so we decided to stay two nights. We were delighted to be reaping the benefit of two managers who seemed to appear as if by magic!

Unfortunately the refurbishment was so recent that Barbara discovered that the 'hot-and-cold' in the new ensuite only came in 'hot' and was gushing anywhere and everywhere – including into the toilet. When we rang reception we were gently told with the wry amusement we came to associate with the Irish, that the plumber must have made a mistake when connecting the taps. We couldn't complain: that gentle Irish humour, the warm hospitality and the slow pace of life beguiled us. Even the porter who carried our cases slowly said that he had spent time in London, but disliked the way everyone spent so much time looking at their watches so had decided to return to Ireland.

We continued our tour, driving around the Ring of Kerry and The Dingle Peninsula to a bed and breakfast hotel, where we were told that if we went to the top of the hill at midday we would be able to watch dolphins jump out of the water below: a regular site for locals.

While in Dingle we had one of those conversations with the kind of happy ramifi-cations that could only occur in Ireland. We met a man in a coffee bar who heard that I was a songwriter and musician and suggested that we should travel a little further on to a village called Camp. He gave us the address of a Tralee Radio broadcaster,

Maire Begley O Seaghdha, whom he thought would be interested to hear my songs.

So, the next day, rather intrigued, we drove on to Camp, and after settling into our accommodation and eating our supper we found the address we had been given and knocked on the door. Maire's husband answered and explained that Maire was at the radio station. But he invited us in to meet his three children, one of whom was a bright young pianist. The piano was very out of tune, so according to my holiday habit, I offered to tune it while Barbara chatted to the family. As it was getting late with still no sign of Maire we arranged to return the following morning.

Our welcome the next day was an especially warm one, after all we were now old friends, and we spent the rest of the morning exchanging music tapes, listening to Maire's accordion playing, with her husband on the bodhran (a traditional Irish instrument) and dancing!

After a very happy time together we said our farewells and Barbara and I set off towards Dublin once more, stopping again at Howth. We booked accommodation and a table at The Abbey Tavern in order to enjoy supper and a night's entertainment, as we had promised ourselves.

We ate Lobster Thermidor in the Tavern restaurant which was so good that I called the waiter: "The Irish cook this dish better than the French!" I exclaimed. "That I wouldn't know," he replied, "our chef is French!"

Hilton Hotel, Park Lane, London Nov. 1992. The Toastmaster greeting Barbara and our friend Marjorie from Devon

At the beginning of 1992, Barbara began to have grand mal attacks with the confusion that so often accompanies them. Sadly, they were to continue without relief. She also began to feel increasingly depressed, so at the beginning of February I arranged for her to spend a fortnight at Crowhurst, a Christian residential centre known for its calm and tranquil atmosphere.

We shared happier news in the middle of February when Mark and Lotte became engaged and we celebrated with the boys and several friends the following Sunday: altogether there were ten young people in the house.

Their lively company was a tonic for both of us.

In October of that year our friend Marjorie visited from Devon and I arranged for the three of us, with Barbara's sister Helen, to attend the Academy Awards lunch at the Hilton Hotel in Park Lane.

On the day itself, I drove into the rear entrance of the hotel as if I had done so every day of my life and Marjorie thought we were simply going somewhere rather grand for coffee. We began by taking in the panoramic sights from the rooftop restaurant where we had a bird's eye view of the changing of the Guard at Buckingham Palace.

Afterwards I led the ladies into the reception hall where 400 of my fellow songwriters and composers and their guests had gathered for pre-lunch drinks. Marjorie was rather nervous, thinking we had gate-crashed somebody else's special event, especially when she spotted a few well known faces. So, tongue in cheek, I nonchalantly explained that we had come to join the lunch party for exactly the same reason as all the 'other' celebrities present: she was dumbstruck.

As we entered the dining room the Toast Master announced the names of the guests and greeted the ladies with a kiss on the hand. This greatly impressed Helen who was totally overwhelmed by the occasion. The Toast Master quipped that the Academy Awards lunch was the only occasion before which he took a bath! (I bet he says that to all the ladies at all the awards lunches...)

In November, Barbara and I went to Sorrento. Barbara particularly needed a peaceful holiday, so we decided not to let the family know we were in Italy.

We stayed in five star luxury – at low season prices – at the stunning Sorrento Palace Hotel, with its multiple swimming pools and frescoed walls.

We took a slow pace, and as is often our preference, spent time relaxing in the foyer to watch the comings and goings and to listen to the hotel pianist. But, as usual, my ears were in occupational mode even on holiday.

I could hear that the piano was very out of tune and simply couldn't let it remain so. When I sensitively suggested as much to the pianist, he agreed with some sense of frustration, and explained that it had been tuned by a local tuner using a machine and obviously not to a satisfactory standard. He asked if I would be able to tune the piano by hand, and as I had my tools with me – as always – I set to work. Once the job was done, the pianist returned to the keys to try out the restored instrument. He was so impressed that he asked me to tune the Bosendorfer at his own home, nearby.

Barbara, by now well used to my accidental tuning assignments on holiday, enjoyed the view over the bay of Sorrento with the pianist's wife, while I worked.

Our tour guide suggested that we all go to The Foreigner's Club for dinner, where I couldn't help noticing that the Italian diners received a far better meal than the somewhat Anglicised Italian food that we tourists were offered: I wasn't impressed!

On another evening, a group of us couldn't resist trying Mario's, a restaurant in town, where we were served with wine. As Barbara can't drink alcohol, I asked the waiters, in Italian, to serve her a non-alcoholic drink. On hearing my Italian, the owner turned to his staff and said, in Neapolitan dialect he didn't think I would understand, "There's an Italian here: we'll have trouble tonight." Of course, he didn't know that I had learned the Neapolitan dialect all those years before, but my fellow guests soon found out that I had and were very amused by my translation. We almost felt like ganging up to give him the 'trouble' he expected!

During the course of the week I had a strong impression that I should ring my Mother. Following my instinct, I was shocked to learn that she was in hospital in Bari. Barbara and I agreed that we should abandon our plans for peace and quiet and hire a car in order to visit her. She was so pleased to see us, albeit briefly. We weren't able to stay with her for long as we had to drive the 150 miles back to Sorrento in order to return the car by the agreed time.

In June of 1993 we visited the Isle of Lewis in Scotland to try to trace Jessie, one of Barbara's former Dickens and Jones colleagues. She had married an Islander and, as far as we knew, still lived on the island. We stayed in Stornoway on our first night and the following morning went in search of Barbara's friend.

In a coffee shop we found somebody who assured us that Jessie and Duncan – her husband – still lived nearby. We hired a car and found the house, and while I sat in the car Barbara went to the door and knocked. When Jessie opened it, she didn't recognise Barbara at first, but as soon as Barbara introduced herself her expression changed to one of delight and she invited us both in and introduced us to her husband.

We stayed for tea and were able to see them both once more before returning home. The friendship renewed, Jessie and Duncan stayed with us for a holiday the following September and we subsequently attended the weddings of their sons.

We continued our Scottish holiday with a visit to the Isle of Harris, famous for its tweed cloth. We found accommodation in Tarbert, the 'capital', spent time on the beautiful white sandy beach – although it was far too cold to swim – and watched, fascinated, as peat diggers piled up peat to dry out before taking it home for their fires.

On Skye we headed west to see Dunveagn Castle and the glorious sunsets.

The Drambuie pancakes I ate for dessert that evening left me more than content and I was able to enjoy the Ceilidh that followed with some abandon!

Leaving Skye, we crossed to the mainland at Mallaig and caught a bus to Fort William. Accommodation was scarce, but eventually we found a guest house with the help of a taxi driver. We drove along the banks of Loch Ness, hoping to spot the monster, but, like most visitors gave up, disappointed. We then took a bus to Oban, whose landscape I found particularly beautiful, from where we crossed to the Isle of Mull. We hired a car at Craignure and drove west to Iona, the remote place of Christian pilgrimage. From there we returned to Mull and, eventually, to Glasgow for our flight home, still moved by the remote beauty of our Scottish holiday.

Later that summer, Barbara began to have problems with her balance. She would suddenly go into a 'spin' which she was unable to control and which left her very confused and shaken. She also suffered added petit or grand mal attacks. Whilst we had become accustomed to the blackouts, the new spinning symptoms were very disturbing. We both hoped that the symptoms would be temporary, but they gradually became worse. When she tried to walk unaided she had to hold out both arms to get her balance as if walking on a tightrope, attracting some curious looks from passers-by!

Barbara's health was helped when she had something to look forward to, not least, Mark and Lotte's wedding which was arranged for 30th October.

Invitations were sent out and arrangements began to be made.

Lotte's father and his partner Lesley invited Barbara and I – with Isa and her mother Cesaria, who happened to be staying with us – to dinner at their beautiful converted barn near Henley on Thames. The dinner was elegantly presented in a very English style and Cesaria began to understand why Isa enjoyed being in England so much!

As a prelude to the wedding, we shared in the Sunday service at St Mary's Church in Hampton and on the evening before the wedding, threw a special pre-wedding supper for a group of very special friends including Glenys, Marjorie and John, Isa and Cesaria. It was a particularly joyful evening and the perfect way to launch a weekend of family celebration.

The wedding was conducted by a lovely female priest, Kitty Platt, who joined us later for the buffet reception held at York House, Twickenham with nearly 200 guests and a live band. Lotte's stepfather Trevor, who has a fine voice, sang 'O Sole Mio' and I added some other Italian songs. It was a great conclusion to a very happy day.

Cesaria, meanwhile, had been so impressed by the quality of the English meat served at the reception, that when she returned to Italy a few days later her bags were filled with a selection of cuts from the local butcher! I would love to have seen the expressions on the faces of the airport security staff who checked those bags!

In February of 1994, Barbara was well enough for us to fly to Boston to celebrate my Aunt Catherine's 90th birthday, with the boys and Lotte joining us a few days later.

The temperature was ten degrees below zero with snow on the ground, but despite the freezing conditions, 130 Italian friends and relatives managed to be present. It was a typical Italian gathering: laughter, good food, lively conversation and a real sense of the celebration of family.

The boys and Lotte returned to England the following Monday, while Barbara and I went on to Los Angeles to stay with our friends Tom and Bridget.

Tom met us at the airport and drove us to their home, which appeared to be situated on a particularly long road: their house-number was 28,987!

Tom and Bridget were unable to take us sightseeing as they both worked, so we arranged to hire a car. A short time after contacting the hire company a beautiful girl arrived at the door with a limousine to take us to the hire company's office where we were left with a slightly smaller vehicle: a Nissan!

It took me about half an hour to master the unfamiliar controls and the American road system, but with my confidence growing and with more than a little bravado and determination, we set off for Hollywood, North of Los Angeles.

Eventually, perhaps miraculously, we arrived at Universal Studios to absorb the whole film studio experience: Jaws; the making of E.T.; sets for Westerns; a demonstration of a gunfight; the (simulated!) effect of an earthquake and the shower set from Psycho, complete with the old house on the hill, which gave me something of an uneasy feeling.

We left Hollywood late in the evening, travelling south and were able to admire the lights of the Los Angeles skyline. Somehow we managed to find our way back to Tom and Bridget's to share tales of our exciting day.

The following morning we drove along the Pacific coast stopping at Newport, a wealthy area characterized by limousine cavalcades – and a large number of police – and on the next, enjoyed the fishy sights of Sea World at San Diego.

On the way home from San Diego we visited friends we had met in Assisi years earlier: Marianne is German, but she produced the best Spaghetti Puttanesca I have ever eaten. So good, in fact, that I demolished three helpings! Whether it was the spaghetti overload, the diversions due to earthquake damage, or the indistinguishable local street scenery, I'm not sure, but we had some trouble finding our way back to Tom and Bridget's that night!

Keen to see the phenomenon that is Las Vegas, we decided to leave Tom and Bridget's for a few days to head for the Nevada desert and the bright lights of 'The Strip'. I booked a stay for

On the terrazzo of the Pensione "Lisa", Rimini, July 1993. Mario & Renato from Rome entertaining the resident guests

the two of us at Caesar's Palace Hotel, and we took the 400 mile journey by car: a strange experience, as the few petrol stations en route inevitably leave a driver uneasy.

On our arrival a valet parked our car and we went to our room, which was enormous. It had two entrances to the bathroom and a shower which shot water at its user from all directions: very disconcerting, especially when it was unexpected.

The next morning, Barbara and I began to explore the hotel and soon realised that it was all under cover. Without natural daylight or sun, different kinds of weather and atmospheric conditions – thunderstorms, sunsets, and midnight – are simulated, so that gamblers will stay longer to spend their money.

There were indoor 'roads' lined with shops – Versace and Armani included – which made us feel as if we were in Rome.

Lunch, for a mere six dollars, gave us any amount of top quality food, and free drinks were constantly offered by Bunny Girl waitresses. Trolleys full of money were always on the move from A to B and the male members of staff were dressed as Romans!

We loved the 'OTT' atmosphere and wanted to stay another night. But despite the 3000 rooms there were no vacancies. So we found another room nearby at the Tropicana, and while Barbara, tired from all the excitement, slept, I explored the other hotels. I discovered the Luxor in the shape of a pyramid; The Excalibur with its knights in armour and The Pirate whose special effects displays simulated a sea battle and sank a ship only for it to reappear to fight another day!

On our way back to Tom and Bridget's home in Los Angeles, it poured with rain and I wondered who it was who said that it never rains in California.

It was the last night of our stay in the USA so we had much to talk about and reflect upon. During the evening we met a friend of Tom and Bridget's who drove a limousine and discovered that he was taking his mother-in-law to the airport the next day for the very same flight as ours. So we arranged for him to take us too, leaving the hire car behind. Consequently, we arrived for our homeward flight in true Hollywood style, eventually reaching London rejuvenated- and ready to face the dull March weather.

In June, my mother's Jehovah's Witness friends in Italy telephoned to tell me that she was becoming particularly frail and forgetful. They had looked after her wonderfully, but felt that they were no longer able to provide the care she needed in her own home. So in July we travelled to Italy to find a residential home that would suit her needs and to arrange the finances to cover the cost. The wheels of Italian bureaucracy usually grind slowly, so I had to make it clear that I only had a limited amount of time in the country. With the help of my mother's friends and some well-informed secretarial help, we received confirmation of a pension subsidy within a few days. We were able to settle her into a residential home where she was surrounded by people we had both known since my childhood.

As we were leaving my mother turned to me and said, "Spero che sono stata una buona madre per voi": 'I hope I've been a good Mum', which touched me greatly. Of course she had.

The circle of life wonderfully continues and we arrived back in England to the happy news that Lotte and Mark were expecting their first child: our first Grandchild.

By sad contrast, on 25th August a call from Italy told me that my Mother had passed away. We arranged to fly to Rome the following morning and drove down to Cassano where the funeral was held that afternoon. Anthony and Mark made their own travel arrangements and were on the same flight. David was in Hungary and sadly unable to be with us.

After four hours of sharing the driving across Italy, Anthony and I arrived exhausted with little time to change into our formal clothes before the funeral. There were 200 people waiting for us at the Kingdom Hall and the whole service was carried out according to my Mother's wishes. I was so grateful for all they had done for her.

David later reminded me of a particularly poignant family time we had shared some months earlier. It was the last time that all the brothers had been together with my Mother in Italy. Somehow or other, we had found ourselves gathering around her tiny figure with my guitar, and began to sing to her. A mix of pride, amusement and embarrassment shone in her eyes. She was, indeed, 'una buona madre'.

Cassano, 1991. Proud Nonna Alessandra with David & Anthony

116

CHAPTER ELEVEN

Emilia Salta! (Jumping Emilia)

Barbara and I had heard much about the Scottish Hogmanay that hearsay combined with our enjoyment of our previous Scottish travels to Loch Lomond, encouraged us to go North of the Border to try the 'Scottish New Year's Eve' for ourselves.

One of my customers was a Glaswegian who generously offered to lend me his entire Scottish costume: kilt, jacket, socks and a big buckled leather belt. Unfortunately he couldn't remember where he had put his sporran despite the fact that he had left some money in it, a rare oversight indeed for a Scot!

He belonged to a church in Staines where some members of the congregation were my customers. News that Mario would soon be attired in a skirt and socks very quickly got around. Everyone was intrigued to know if I was really going to wear the kilt and asked what I was going to wear beneath it, to which I replied 'something flaming red!'

As 1994 drew to a close, Barbara and I travelled to Edinburgh by rail to stay at The Sheraton Hotel. As our train pulled in at Waverley Station it was bustling with students from all over the world, many arriving home in time for Hogmanay.

The following day, after breakfasting on kippers, we took an open-top bus tour of the city and then explored on foot, covering the Royal Mile and window shopping in Princes Street. We stopped to gaze up at the Old Town and the Castle towering above us and listened to the lone piper playing his bagpipes – so much loved by Barbara – on the corner by the Scott Monument.

On New Years' Eve we dressed for the Big Bash with me in the borrowed kilt (with flaming

Sheraton Hotel 31 December 1994.
Mario & Barbara celebrating Hogmanay with 2 same table party goers

red beneath!). I may have looked suitably dashing, but Barbara was far more beautiful, in a green velvet dress with a tartan sash secured by a large brooch.

Whilst sipping the champagne that gave a suitable start the evening, I heard some Italian voices and turned to introduce myself to a gentleman who turned out to be the Italian Consul. He asked if I had been born in Edinburgh, or indeed if I was at all Scottish. When I answered, 'No' he asked why I was wearing a kilt, to which I replied 'When in Rome...' the irony of which caused some amusement.

Dinner was a very grand affair, with two bands playing us through the evening, until the moment came when the Haggis was piped in and the Robbie Burns' recited. I was fascinated by the whole proceedings, almost betraying the apparent familiarity and nonchalance implied by my kilt.

We spent the rest of the night – or early morning – joining in with the vigorous Scottish dancing. Then everyone was served with beef tea as a night cap. As I sipped my beefy brew I chatted to a young Scottish woman and asked her if she knew what Hogmanay meant. She confessed that many Scottish people didn't know and neither – to her shame – did she. So I was able to tell her that it means 'Hug me now!' to which she replied "Trust you, you're an Italian – you would say that, wouldn't you?!"

The following day the hotel served an enormous buffet brunch and in the evening we were surprised by the arrival of David and Andrea who suddenly appeared to announce their engagement. It was the perfect end to a fabulous New Year and we invited them to join us for dinner to celebrate.

At the end of February, Barbara and I went for a long weekend to the Blundellsands Hotel in Great Cosby, Liverpool. Barbara was reminded of happy times with Auntie Marjorie during the war, and was able to fulfill her long-held wish to stay in the hotel.

In April we celebrated the birth of our first Grandchild, Emilia – Millie for short, to Mark and Lotte. It was quite a novelty to have a baby girl in the family!

During a short trip to Italy in April we stopped at the farm in Faenza to visit Lucia (Domenico's mother), traveling on

Barlow Road, Hampton Dec. 98.
Grandchildren Millie & Tullio showing an
appreciation of piano playing

to stay with Isa and Cesaria's family in Acquaviva. We took Lucia back to England with us by car at the end of April, and as she so enjoyed music, I arranged several musical events for her. On one evening three opera singers came to our home for a musical evening, including Trevor, Lotte's stepfather, who had sung at Mark and Lotte's wedding. Lucia had tears in her eyes as she listened to the singing and was moved by the warm welcome she had received.

Her visit was over all too soon and as Lucia reluctantly contemplated her first flight she complained that if she wanted to get home she supposed she would have to fly. In fact, much to her surprise she thoroughly enjoyed the experience.

In June, Barbara was well enough to travel so we both joined a coach trip organised by the Piano Tuners Association with the intention of visiting the major piano factories across Europe.

Hamburg was the first stop: a beautiful city with a vast lake at its very centre. After settling into our hotel we visited the Steinway factory and began to appreciate the high level of workmanship that goes into the making of these famous instruments. The next day we were free to visit the city so we took the bus, visiting beautifully decorated churches and passing the multi-layered railway station with its multitude of small cafes and shops.

The following day we travelled to Braunschweig to see the Shimmell factory before going on to Berlin to see where Bechsteins are made.

We visited the Brandenburg Gates and took a tour of Berlin before going on to Heidelberg, Stuttgart, Ruddesheim and Leipzig where we visited the Bluthner factory. Mr. Bluthner and his son showed us around the factory and helped us to understand the source of the soft tonal quality that makes these pianos so popular: Bluthners are the piano tuners favourite as they respond so well to tuning. Mr. Bluthner explained that the factory was about to produce the 150,000th piano and that there was some debate as to whom it would be most appropriate to present as a gift. Perhaps a head of state or a famous musician? Some years later, I met Mr. Bluthner again in Italy, and he told me that the piano was eventually donated to The Leipzig Academy of Music. Who could be more appropriate for the receipt of such a piano than talented music students?

The following day we travelled to Dresden and were moved and impressed by the regeneration of this once devastated city and the few beautiful buildings still left standing following the air raids of the 1939-1945 war.

Prague was our next stop, and the Petroff piano factory.

Our visit to Prague was sadly overshadowed when Barbara's purse was stolen as she walked between the sliding doors of an underground train. Her purse – minus notes – was rescued from a waste bin, but our house keys were taken, which particularly disconcerted Barbara. No progress was made with the police and there was little that could be done, despite my attempt to confront the thief and his child assistant who, to our astonishment, remained at the scene. At dinner that evening we discovered that our experience was common to several of our companions. The dinner itself did little to cheer any of us up or transform our memories of Prague. But the meal we enjoyed at the Petroff factory the following day did raise our spirits. It was cooked in the factory kitchen, which, curiously, had been sponsored by a piano importer from Dorset. It was simple, wholesome and quite delicious.

Our next destination was Vienna, where we stayed at The Holiday Inn, and where the hotel food became more reliable. We visited the Bosendorfer factory and the Schonbrum Palace, set in beautiful gardens. We wandered through the elegant rooms and emerged into a huge ballroom with an ornate ceiling. Noticing a piano in one corner, covered with a dust sheet, it was inevitable that a group of piano tuners would want to discover the make of an instrument located in such a grand setting. How disappointed we were to discover that this instrument was not a local Bosendorfer or even a German piano, it was Japanese!

On the final day we visited Salzburg, where our faith in German music making was restored amongst the rich heritage of Mozart's home: the perfect end to our musical tour.

Anthony, at this time, was working for Barclays Bank as a business analyst. His working locations were often arduous: on one occasion he was sent to the Cayman Islands where he stayed in a beautiful hotel only twenty metres from the beach. We all agreed it was a tough job, but somebody had to do it.

In November he was asked to go to New York for three months, so Barbara and I took the opportunity to visit him and see something of The Big Apple. We crossed the Atlantic in December to stay in some style in Anthony's spacious Manhattan apartment which came complete with a concierge and its own view of the Statue of Liberty.

We visited the twin towers – now a poignant memory – and spent time with friends from Cassano at their apartment in Harrison. We enjoyed a meal in a Pugliese restaurant in the Italian quarter and amused ourselves simply people-watching in the large reception area of the Marriott Hotel.

One morning, while Anthony was at work, we set off on foot to explore the city. We walked past the Dow Jones building heading for Wall Street from where we planned to catch the subway to Bloomingdales.

Barbara, wrapped up against the cold in her Icelandic hat, suddenly tripped and fell. She was immediately surrounded by a group of ladies – one of whom was a doctor – asking if they could help. I couldn't help mentioning how pleasantly surprised I was, as I had heard that New Yorkers had a reputation for simply stepping over anyone who fell! The doctor explained that they were not New Yorkers, but Texans, visiting New York to do their Christmas shopping! We all enjoyed the joke and went our separate ways. Barbara was reassured that if she ever fell over in Texas, help would be at hand.

We eventually reached New York's most famous department store each in one piece, but I considered Bloomingdales Christmas windows a poor reflection of Harrods. Or perhaps I was biased? Nevertheless, we did a little Christmas shopping and got chatting to another friendly Texan over a cup of tea. She told us that she was in New York to spend her Grandchildren's inheritance, an expression I hadn't heard before, but which I now use myself-often.

My cousin Geno had told us that he was going to be at the Metropolitan Opera House in New York the next day, to queue for a book signing by the opera singer Renata Tebaldi. Geno is such a great fan that he sends Renata a birthday card every year. We approached the Opera House and spotted Geno tucked away in the queue which was very long. After three hours we finally got to the head. I was able to photograph Renata Tebaldi signing Geno's book and shaking his hand. Dear Geno treasures that photograph.

We decided to leave New York with Geno and fly home from Boston, buying some large red apples to eat on our journey. They were delicious: a perfect tribute to 'The Big Apple.'

After Christmas at home with the family, Barbara and I flew to Edinburgh once again for a Scottish Hogmanay to welcome in the New Year: 1996.

As the spring advanced, it became clear that Barbara's balance was worsening. The doctors at the National Hospital decided to do some tests, including a centrifugal system assessment to see if her problems were connected with fluid in her inner ear. The tests took four hours after which the doctor was able to conclude and explain that the trouble stemmed more from her original brain surgery, thirty years earlier, than from any inner ear problems.

During the latter part of May, Barbara began to have severe pain in her right ear which necessitated return visits to both the National and Kingston hospitals. The skin inside her ear was cracked and bleeding, but with treatment the pain gradually subsided. After so much trauma Barbara suffered several Grand Mal attacks, which continued to be disorientating for Barbara and concerning for all of us.

Happier days were ahead. In September Isa and her sister Francesca came from Italy for David and Andrea's wedding. Friends and

St James Church, Weybridge Surrey.
22 September 1996. David & Andrea's Wedding

family arrived from all over the world to share in the celebrations.

The wedding was held at Weybridge Parish Church, where Andrea's family has worshipped for many years, with a reception afterwards at Hampton Court Palace. About 110 guests sat down to a splendid three course meal and speeches, after which Franco's band entertained us for the evening.

David and Andrea travelled to Thailand for their honeymoon where Andrea, who loves elephants, could see them at close quarters and take a ride.

Just a few weeks later, on the 7th October, there was more happy news with the birth of our second grandchild, Tullio, to Mark and Lotte. I was thrilled to have my own name included in his.

Despite our wide and varied travels, Barbara and I had not yet been on a cruise. So when, in October, Barbara noticed an advertisement in *The Radio Times* for a classical music cruise with Richard Baker, we decided to go.

The planned itinerary included Gibraltar, Spain, Cyprus, Israel and Greece.

We left Southampton on the Oriana on the 16th November among nearly 2000 passengers. The ship was so large that it took us several hours to find our way around from our fourth deck rooms.

We chose the first sitting for dinner each evening in order to be able to make the most of the evening entertainment, and as the Director of Entertainment sat at our table we were often the first to know exactly what that entertainments programme held in store!

Our first port of call was Gibraltar, where most of the passengers stocked up on alcohol as the tax was minimal. Then on to Cyprus, where we were taken up into the hills by coach, stopping at various villages en route, before arriving at a restaurant for a meal of traditional roast lamb.

We sailed overnight, docking at the bustling port of Haifa the following morning.

I had been looking forward to visiting Israel. As there were three options for excursions we chose to go to the River Jordan, The Mount of the Beatitudes and Nazareth.

Our first impressions of the region were of order and tidiness. There was an abundance of fruit and vegetables everywhere and gardens full of vivid colour.

The River Jordan, site of Christ's baptism was an awe inspiring spot, the focal point of centuries of spiritual pilgrimage. On The Mount of the Beatitudes I was especially proud to discover that the church had been built by an Italian!

Nazareth was, by contrast, sadly disappointing. It was crowded with tourists, heavily overbuilt and a far cry from the small and insignificant village it had been in Jesus' day.

We returned to the ship, tired but content and sailed on to Piraievs, near Athens, from where we were taken to the Acropolis, its temples towering above the city on 'The Sacred Hill'.

We spent the three days it took to reach Malaga sunbathing, walking the mile around the deck and enjoying the on board entertainment.

One afternoon we joined a Latin American dance class, and although Barbara was unable to progress very far because of her balance, I did manage to master the cha-cha-cha. The day ended with a Latin American dance so that we could practice our skills and I plucked up the courage to ask one of the duty officers to partner me. Little did I know that she was also a Latin American dance champion: she spun me around the room with great skill until I felt like a champion myself.

The evening before we reached Malaga, we enjoyed an impromptu concert given by passengers at which I played two of my own compositions.

Although it was November, we had enjoyed exceptionally good weather on board ship but arrived back in grey England on the 2nd December: the twins' birthday. It was strange being back on terra firma and took us several days to settle back into our normal routine.

Our dear friend Conrad Leonard celebrated his 100th birthday the following October with a lively party. Franco and I were asked to play 'Happy Birthday' as Conrad was presented with a specially iced birthday cake. The celebrations continued the following Sunday with a reception in the elegant and formal surroundings of the Plaisterers Company Hall in the City of London, where we were entertained by opera singer friends of Conrad's and by a pianist who played one of Conrad's own compositions.

Perhaps Conrad's example renewed my inspiration and ambition, because following a trip to Boston to visit my Aunt Caterina and her family, I returned to record two of my songs to enter the Eurovision Song Contest, hoping for wider recognition.

As I was working on the project, our grandson Daniel was born to Andrea and David on the 2nd December sharing his birthday with his dad and his uncle: we now have three birthdays to celebrate on that same day!

As I needed a female singer for the songs I had written, one of my customers introduced me to a girl called Tari Moore who had just the voice to interpret them. With Franco on saxophone we made a recording with very pleasing results. Unfortunately the songs didn't go forward for the contest, but there was some good news for Franco and Tari by way of consolation.

While Franco was playing at The Elephant on the River one evening, an industrialist and hotelier from Tobago heard his band play and very much liked

Tobago Pigeon Point Feb. 2001. Mario climbing down after picking a coconut

their style. He offered Franco a booking at his hotel in Tobago on full pay and expenses for six to eight weeks. This was obviously an opportunity not to be missed, and as they needed a singer too, Tari was suggested.

Franco and the band, with Tari in tow, flew to Tobago for their extended working holiday at the end of December.

I eagerly followed the progress of Franco and his musician friends, wondering if perhaps their Caribbean experience would be difficult to endure.

After all, they were required to play each evening for two or three hours and spent most of the day on the beautiful white beaches of Tobago. Concerned as I was for my brother in this hardship, I felt I should check out his level of overwork. As our friends Reg and Christine offered to have Barbara to stay with them for a week, I flew out to Tobago to investigate.

I stayed in Franco's room in a convenient spare bed and spent a week sharing the hardships of sun, sea, good food and good company, returning satisfied that my brother was not too exploited.

Sadly, Barbara's moods and behaviour began to change as she became more confused and much more inclined to sleep. Family and friends suggested that it might be helpful for her to be seen by a neuro-psychiatrist at The Priory, a private hospital in Roehampton.

We detailed her previous surgery and treatments for the medical team and explained that she had been treated at The Royal Marsden and The National Hospital for Neurosurgery: two of the best hospitals in the country.

When the doctor in charge had gathered all the details of tests and consultations, he admitted that sadly he would not be able to improve her condition, but promised to send a full report of his assessment in a few days. This concluded that Barbara was suffering from an organic brain disease and it was unlikely that her condition would improve.

We became all the more determined to enjoy our usual programme of visits, friends and concerts, as much and as long as Barbara was able.

Partying seemed the best way forward! So in December, as I approached the fortieth anniversary of my cold, foggy arrival in England, complete with stuffed rabbit and Long Johns, we decided to celebrate by inviting friends and relatives to a celebration.

We set up two very long tables in the lounge and covered them with cloths, decorating the room around them.

We had recently employed a young Polish girl, Margaret, as a cleaner so I asked her to help me in the kitchen on the night. I told her that we should not allow anyone else to help as I wanted them to enjoy the party. Margaret took this very much as her personal responsibility and defended the kitchen as if it was my personal bank vault. And she didn't stop working for a moment. In the end I had to be very firm to get her to stop washing up and clearing plates long enough to share some food!

We all enjoyed a hot buffet of lasagna and cannelloni, reminiscences, music and laughter (there wasn't a stuffed rabbit in sight).

Mark and family had visited New Zealand and Australia in 2000 and in January 2001, decided to move with a pregnant Lotte to Sydney. Our fourth grandson was born in May and was called Matteo Anthony Osborne ("Oz-born") but sadly due to Barabara's ill health, we were unable to visit. Mark and family did attend Rosa & Saverio's 50th Wedding Anniversary in Adelaide, with their two children and new baby, on our behalf to bring some champagne.

Barbara was still able to get out and about to a limited extent, so as she is very fond of the opera singer, Lesley Garrett, I ordered some tickets for a concert later that month – and hoped to add an extra surprise.

I wrote to Ms.Garrett's agent to ask if I could arrange for Barbara to meet the singer. To my delight she agreed, and said that she would meet us after the concert and take us to Miss Garrett's dressing room. In the event we met Lesley, as she sashayed her way elegantly along the corridor towards us, on her way to a party. She stopped, greeted us and took time to talk to Barbara posing for a photograph with us all: Barbara was thrilled.

After a quiet Christmas and New Year we received an invitation to the wedding of our friend Fiona in Perth, Australia.

As Barbara was starting to find travel difficult we decided that I should go alone. It seemed a sad point to have reached after all our travels together, but Barbara would not have me miss out. So I made plans to spend two weeks in Australia, attending the wedding in Perth and then moving on to visit my sister Rosa and her husband Saverio, in Adelaide.

For Barbara, I arranged a rather different holiday: a stay in Brinsworth House in Twickenham, where artists, entertainers and their families are accommodated for rest and recuperation. I felt that if she was going to be entertained anywhere, it may as well be where there were professional entertainers!

I flew to Perth on a cold and grey day at the end of February to be met by sunshine and blues skies, and Fiona, who drove me around the city for an introductory tour.

At that time, she and Scott lived very close to Western Australia University where she lectured, but I was to stay with Tom and Bridget, who had exchanged their house in (rainy) Los Angeles for a house in Perth for three months.

I expected an easy start to my stay and slow recuperation from the long haul flight, but the following morning I had a surprise wake up call at 7.30. It was Tom inviting me to go for an early morning swim in the Indian Ocean. It seemed an offer too good to refuse – even with jet lag. So after an exhilarating start to the day we enjoyed a cappuccino in an Italian bar and went back to the house for breakfast.

Before supper that evening, while I helped Fiona in the kitchen, Tom went into town to buy Chianti in my honour, to go with our Italian meal. As Fiona and I chopped, stirred and chatted, she asked me if I would pull a bottle of wine from the wine rack to ease our preparations along. It was a very pleasant Australian Shiraz –

On board of a boat, taking the bride & groom, friends and relatives on the Swan River, Perth, W.A. 2.3.2000. Mario & Bride Fiona

and I was converted. When Tom returned triumphantly holding the Chianti he had searched long and hard for, I asked if I could carry on drinking the Shiraz, much to Bridget and Fiona's amusement. Was I a traitor to my own cause?

The next morning we gathered at Scott and Fiona's home, to prepare for the wedding, where I was introduced to the family, one of whom I could hardly take my eyes off: a striking, elegant woman in dark glasses had joined the party. She was immaculately dressed and mildly mysterious and reminded me of Ava Gardner. But alas, she turned out to be Scott's mother!

The wedding ceremony was held in the beautiful sunken garden of the university with music provided by a string trio. Afterwards we sailed on the Black Swan River as champagne flowed and a lavish dinner was served, dancing until the small hours. I thought of Barbara so far away and hoped she had found someone to dance with too.

The fun continued the following day as I joined a party on a sailing trip to Rot's Next Island.

We moored offshore where I was encouraged to dive, rather than jump, into the deep water. I'm not much of a diver, so I jumped – and sunk speedily towards the bottom. I was swiftly rescued by Fiona and her sister Catherine.

Being rescued by two bikini clad beauties meant I thought I had died and gone to heaven.

I calmed down with a gentle swim and some sunbathing before we all returned to shore to sit outside a coffee bar on Cappuccino Street. As its name suggests, Cappuccino Street is lined with Italian bars and restaurants, with mostly Italian staff.

As we enjoyed our coffee, I chatted to the waiters, most of whom were young Italians born in Australia.

"Do you wish you were back in Italy?" I asked. But they assured me that they were quite happy "apart from missing Italian football."

The following day I flew to Adelaide to complete my Australian holiday by spending a few days with Rosa and Saverio. Most of those I had left behind in Perth were tall, fair, Anglo-Saxons, so it was something of a contrast to be met by my family: a group of small, dark, southern Italians!

The final days of my Australian trip were spent in long conversations with much loved family in a fruit and vine filled garden. It was hard to wrench myself away to return to London.

In the middle of June, Barbara felt well enough to travel in familiar terrain, so Geno arrived from Boston to accompany us to Italy. We spent time in Faenza, Rimini and in Cassano, staying at the hill-top Hotel Ulivo.

We then drove on to Rome to stay at our favourite Hotel, The Lancelot. The hotel had been refurbished, and when Geno saw that the bathroom contained a combined lavatory and bidet he murmured, 'Trust the Romans to think of such a clever design!'

We stayed in Rome for five days, and while Geno dashed around the city taking in the Vatican and the historical sights, Barbara and I took a slower pace, ambling gently around the shops and sitting by the Trevi fountain, beautifully cool on a hot day. At suppertime we enjoyed some lively company: two Cuban lady doctors, a Danish gentleman, a gentleman from Finland and two ladies from Belgium, such is the international appeal of Rome!

In September, Barbara had an appointment at The National Neurological Hospital for a review. But she was more interested in the way her consultant, Professor Cipollati, rushed from place to place on his motorbike, or carrying his helmet, than she was in his comments about her health.

An MRI scan a week or so later proved negative, but she was still showing signs of poor balance and loss of memory. Her medical team confirmed that these symptoms were the result of surgery in the sixties and radiotherapy in the seventies, and repeated that unfortunately she would not improve.

But Christmas was a happy family affair, as ever, and Barbara and I made another of our much loved Hogmanay trips to Edinburgh, this time to stay at The Carlton Hotel. Its position on the North Bridge, meant that just before midnight we were able to gather with other guests on the bridge to watch the firework display as it danced across the city skies. The crowd around us was made up of people from all over the world and was extremely well-behaved-even the Italians!

At about the same time Franco and his band left for a repeat of his arduous Tobago hotel booking, this time joined by the band's resident singer, Maureen.

Concerned once again about Franco's hard labour in the Caribbean, I decided to join him to help out; leaving Barbara well cared for at Brinsworth House.

When I arrived in Tobago I discovered that Maureen, the band's singer, was to be

Elephant on the River, London April 2001. Barbara fascinated on listening to the Piper playing Amazing Grace on our fortieth anniversary

married on the beach to Robin, her fiancé, and to my delight, she asked me to give her away.

As I met Maureen at the end of the road leading to the beach, to walk her to her wedding, it became apparent that this tall, blond woman of 5ft 8"(including heels) towered over my 5ft 4" figure, making us something of an odd couple!

But Maureen is a resourceful young woman and spotted a solution: she quickly removed her shoes and jump-stepped sideways to a slightly lower level of the beach to even up our height. As Franco played 'Here comes the bride' on the saxophone we approached the wedding party as if our 'tall and small' approach was completely normal.

It was late in the day, and as the minister gave what was an interesting but rather long address we noticed that the tide was coming in. He assured us that getting our feet wet on such a day would only bring good luck!

Everyone joined in the celebrations with a moving rendition of 'Amazing Grace', our voices floating out across the sea.

In March, Barbara and I celebrated our fortieth wedding anniversary with a family buffet party at The Elephant on the River. There were about forty of us, including Franco's band and the newly married Maureen and her husband – who sang 'Amazing Grace' once again. To Barbara's delight this was followed by a Scottish piper playing the same tune on his bagpipes, reminding us of very many happy trips to Scotland.

Our friend Vanessa gave a moving speech and read the apostle Paul's eternal words about love from 1 Corinthians 13.

My 65th birthday the following June was celebrated with another party, and the completion of our mortgage! Our first little maisonette in Colliers Wood seemed a very long time ago.

I think of you

With Barbara's condition deteriorating and her prognosis unchanging, life became increasingly challenging.

We had married for better for worse and pledged our faithfulness in sickness and in health, but we could never have imagined the degree to which those vows would be words to live by on a daily basis.

At the end of July a tumour was discovered on Barbara's ovaries and she was admitted to hospital for a hysterectomy followed by weekly sessions of radiotherapy at The Royal Marsden.

Shortly afterwards, The National Neurological Hospital arranged for her to have another MRI scan and a subsequent examination by a neuro-psychiatrist. Once again we were told that there was little that could be done to improve her situation.

Our family continued to give us much joy and a sense of purpose and optimism which helped us both through the difficult days.

In the summer of 2001, Anthony introduced us to Khine, a lovely Burmese girl, to her daughter Bali and to her uncle Tin, who all joined us for dinner.

The next January 2002, our grandson Nathan Benedetto was born to Andrea and David, to much rejoicing. In March 2002, Anthony received his Masters degree at Birkbeck College in London and Barbara was – wonderfully – well enough to go with me to the ceremony.

In June, as a birthday present to myself and in fulfillment of a long cherished dream, I was able to buy a shiny new Mercedes. I collected it with Franco in order to share the occasion with him. As we drove, we were as excited as we had been as two small boys. We reflected that we had come a long way from those days when we had only our feet to carry us around the streets of Cassano: it was a proud day for both of us.

Anthony and Khine were married in February 2003 and celebrated with a reception at The Elephant on the River: which

The Elephant on the River Thames, February 2003. Anthony & Khine's wedding

was fast becoming our chosen venue for family parties. All three sons were now married – in reverse order – with Anthony following the 'first shall be last' principle!

As Easter 2003 approached, Manuela and Marina and their families invited me to spend the holiday with them on the Isle of Ischia off the coast of Naples.

Once again, Barbara encouraged me to go. So once she was settled in Brinsworth House, I flew out to Italy. I stayed at The Citara Restaurant hotel, whose terrace ran along the edge of the sea, offering stunning views.

Anthony, Khine and Bali joined me, staying in a sister hotel on the hillside.

After spending one day touring the island with them, I set out to walk back to my hotel, talking to Barbara on my mobile phone. Distracted, I missed my footing and went tumbling down onto the rocky ground.

I managed to walk down to the hotel in great pain, where Manuela, who is a doctor, examined me, not realising that my arm was broken. She gave me painkillers and anti-inflammatory tablets and I hoped for the best.

That evening we went to Forio for a Good Friday procession depicting Christ's walk to the cross and his crucifixion. It was very moving and the drama certainly helped me to forget the pain in my arm, but the next day it was no better, so Anthony and Khine persuaded me to go to the local hospital, where a fracture was diagnosed. A plaster was applied all around my waist and right arm with just my hand in view!

As I recovered, trying to grow accustomed to my strange plaster appendage, I reminded Khine and Anthony that earlier on the day of the accident I had gone shoe shopping with them and had bought a pair of shoes. As we left the shop, Khine had told me that it is the custom in Burma to give new shoes a bite for luck when leaving the shop where they had been bought. So I had done so. 'So much for your custom' I joked. 'I was wearing those shoes when I fell!'

Determined not to let my plastered state inhibit my holiday, Khine arranged their move to a room on the same floor of my hotel so that Anthony could help me dress: something of a comical task!

The following day we rose early to cross the water to the Isle of Capri. A heavy morning mist cleared as we reached the island to climb the hundreds of steps to the top. I watched every one of mine *very* carefully!

I returned to England to be told that my old friend Conrad Leonard had died at the age of 104: we had known him for nearly forty years. His help in recording my music had been invaluable. He had not just been a help-mate and inspiration to me, but a dear friend.

Barbara suffered a fall in June and was taken to Kingston Hospital, where it soon became clear that her accident had caused complications to her condition, as she didn't recognise me. When Mark and his daughter Millie arrived, Barbara kept asking for an ice-cream from Selfridges, so Mark did his best. He couldn't quite make Selfridges, but found an ice-cream locally. On his return Barbara didn't want the ice-cream and didn't recognise Mark, going on to ask Millie if she was 37 years old, much to Millie's amusement!

Fortunately, Barbara's memory returned in a few days, but the hospital team decided to keep her in for a while for observation.

A report was sent to The National Neurological Hospital who then admitted her for a full series of examinations. She spent over three weeks in hospital, at the end of which I was told that she was in the early stages of dementia caused by the earlier surgery and radiotherapy: it had left her with irreparable mild brain damage. We were advised that it was important that the whole family understand the implications of the diagnosis; particularly that Barbara may need specialist residential care at some time in the future. We could only hope to delay that time as long as possible.

My spirits were lifted on 19th July when I was asked to tune the piano of Sophie Raworth, the BBC News reader, for her engagement party. I have known Sophie since her teens as her mother was one of my customers. I was delighted when Sophie was at the house to greet me when I arrived.

Meanwhile, our good friend Don had expressed a request to experience 'the everyday life of Italians', so we planned a trip for August. I told him he would not be disappointed!

A few weeks later, Barbara changed her 'hotel' to St Mary's Residential Home in Hampton and Don and I flew to Rome to drive south.

We stopped at Caserta to see the *Reggia*, once the summer residence of the king of Naples, an extensive, sumptuous, palace surrounded by three miles of gardens.

We continued our journey, crossing to Ischia and the Hotel Cittara where I had stayed the previous Easter. We then caught the ferry to Naples, driving towards the Amalfi coast, enjoying the stunning views at every twist and turn.

We arrived in Acquaviva just in time to watch the medieval costumed cavalcade.

This procession takes place three days before the main festival to St Mary of Constantinople, the town's patron saint, and is a riot of noise and excitement.

Young people on horseback jostle their mounts close together; flag throwers shoot swathes of colour into the air, catching them skilfully and drummers stagger under the weight of huge drums, thumping out a constant beat. We watched enthralled as the parade trailed its way slowly through the streets. Our timing was perfect and I was

Acquaviva delle Fonti, Italy, September 2003.
Procession of the Madonna of Constantinople

glad that Don was with me to witness such a spectacle.

We stayed with Nicola and Laura's family meaning that their son and daughter, Giuseppe and Marilena, were able to practice their English with Don who taught them to count to a hundred. He also encouraged them to memorise the days of the week and the months of the year. We felt that at least they'd know what day it was whenever they were in England!

The main fiesta celebrations were postponed for twenty four hours because of heavy rain, but they were worth the wait. Hot air balloons moved slowly and laboriously skywards to the roar of flame; brass bands crashed their way through the narrow streets and a late night firework display ended the celebrations in a noisy riot of colour.

We spent the next few days visiting the surrounding towns and villages including Sassi di Matera, the location for Mel Gibson's 'Passion of the Christ'.

The town is a unique maze of stony alleyways and bizarrely shaped buildings and is believed to be one of the first human settlements in Italy. Its unique bank of homes grew in height on one slope of a ravine created by a river which is now a mere stream. Many of the houses – known as 'tufo'- are little more than caverns today, but originally hundreds of dwellings were cut out of the rocks to house what, at one time, had been 58,000 inhabitants.

We returned to England on the 10th September, Don's diary full of accounts of 'The everyday life of Italians'.

To our delight, Barbara was well enough to make the trip to Edinburgh for Hogmanay in December, this time to stay at The Caledonian Hilton.

We toured Edinburgh by car in the afternoon, and as Barbara was feeling so well we looked forward to the evening celebrations. In fact she was so enthusiastic at the sound of a piper playing in the corridor before the festivities began, that she forgot herself, as often happened, and shot out of the room to meet him in her underwear and tights. Her semi clad state greeted not only the piper but several other guests, to embarrassed, if understanding, amusement.

But it wasn't just Barbara who caused blushes.

Shortly after our arrival home, I was asked to share my experiences of Italy during the war at Millie and Tullio's school. After giving my talk to Millie's class I picked up my guitar and began singing 'Ciao Bambina'. As I was sitting opposite Millie's young blond teacher she blushed somewhat, making Millie and her friends giggle. When Millie got home she told her father that I had made her teacher blush, adding 'Just fancy, if Nonno married my teacher she would become my Grandmother!'

Sadly, I was already a married man.

Having celebrated 43 years of that marriage with Barbara, I left her to try out her latest choice of 'hotel': The Lynde House in East Twickenham, while I flew across the globe for another Australian visit.

Fiona met me in Perth and showed me around the district to which she and Scott had recently moved. It was called Sorrento! I felt as if they had chosen it just for me.

Their house backed onto a very large park where there were dozens of species of birds, some capable of varied – and loud – wake up calls.

Fiona would drop me at the ferry so that I could make my way into the centre of town and enjoy wandering around by myself, often eating Australian Fish and Chips!

One afternoon I went to the University where Fiona was teaching and joined her and her colleagues to watch a cricket match. As we sat in the sunshine, beer and sandwiches were brought out and I (almost) felt like an Englishman – even in Australia.

I flew on to Adelaide to be met by my sister, Rosa; my brother-in-law, Saverio; my brother, Enzo; Enzo's wife, Lina and their families. It was good to see them again.

Anthony, Khine and their family were staying with friends in the Blue Mountains so we arranged that they would join us in Adelaide. We spent a happy Easter together by the sea, eating fabulous food and sightseeing.

I flew on to Sydney where I was met by Arthur – my best man – and his wife Maureen who had invited me to stay with them in their home in North Sydney. When I arranged my trip they had told me that they would be delighted to see me as they had a garage full of beer. When I remarked that I only drink wine, they said that they would be sure to fill it with wine instead. I was amused at the thought of much to-ing and fro-ing with boxes and bottles just to satisfy my whim!

Arthur and Maureen took me sightseeing, first to the Sydney Opera House and then on a boat trip round the harbour. I had been given a hat by my brother, Enzo and to make it look like the genuine Australian article I had trimmed the base of the crown with a strip of leather decorated with crocodile teeth: I felt like Crocodile Dundee.

One evening Arthur and Maureen prepared a wonderful fish supper after which I was surprised to be asked by their son Peter's very beautiful wife to teach her some Italian swear words, the naughtier the better. I was very reluctant to do so, but she insisted, so eventually I obliged, to everyone's amusement!

In May 2004, two weeks after my return to England I heard of the death of Cesaria, Isa's mother, after a long illness. I was very sad as Cesaria had been like a sister to me. She was a wonderful dressmaker and when her husband became disabled, worked hard to meet his every need and supported the family by working from home. She would get up at 4am to start work on beautiful special occasion clothes for which she was much in demand. I flew to Acquaviva to attend her funeral on the 8th May.

Back home, work was required. I was finding it hard to get Barbara in and out of the car, so decided to change the layout of the area in front of the house to make access easier. I arranged for a pergola and white picket fence to be built and had the front of the house painted. It looked so smart with its face lift that I felt the need to give our home a name. In the early hours of one morning, I had a flash of inspiration, deciding that it should be 'Ciao', the word Barbara spoke when we met at the top of the aisle on our wedding day: it would give a similar happy greeting to our visitors.

Barlow Road, Hampton, May 2007. Mario & Barbara front garden & "Ciao!" name on the house

After searching in vain for the appropriate letters for the sign, I asked my friend G1, in Acquaviva, if he could help. "Leave it to me" he said.

G1 cut out the letters from a solid piece of brass and promised to visit to fit them over the pergola himself. He brought not only the letters, but a large quantity of parmesan cheese, four litres of red wine and two litres of olive oil.

Friends like G1 are hard to find!

In November I went to Cambridge for a Europiano conference while Barbara's brother, Leslie, stayed with her.

I met Sergio Brunelli, the vice president of Europiano, who told me that as there are no Italian courses in musical instrument technology he was required to learn his skills at a piano factory in Germany. I discovered that as a piano tuner, he travelled from Treviso, his home town, to Venice for two or three days a month, using a gondola to get around!

Sergio asked me what he might take home to Italy to best represent the English celebration of Christmas. I suggested some Christmas crackers and mince pies and heard later that they had gone down very well!

In April, I flew to Boston to visit Geno and his family, taking Elisabetta, G1's daughter, and her boyfriend, Giuseppe, with me.

When Geno's brother Frank discovered that Giuseppe was a policeman in Italy, he arranged a tour of the local police station which would give Giuseppe an understanding of American police prodedure. Giuseppe was given a hat, badges and other mementoes and had his photograph taken with a Boston police car. He was delighted by the whole experience.

We flew to Nashville, via Cincinatti, to be met by another of Geno's brothers, Joe, and the following day were treated to a typical American lunch and a country music show: 'The Grand Old Oprey.'

Catherine, Joe's eldest daughter, and her husband David, invited us to their home, where I tuned the Steinway Grand in their lounge (I was on holiday after all) and swam in their heated pool. Before lunch we were offered cocktails – and large cigars – much to Geno's delight, followed by a very large and delicious fillet of beef which had been marinated for hours.

Giuseppe got on particularly well with Joe's outgoing wife, Carmela. She is of Sicilian origin and still uses some of the old dialect expressions. Joe, at 82 appears to produce a different American breakfast every day and heads out on a three mile walk. One day I joined him for both and greatly enjoyed our conversation.

On the final day of our stay with them, Joe and Carmela took us to The Bluebird Café, a launching pad for would-be country and western singers. Somehow I didn't think my style would fit, so didn't develop any ambition.

We flew on to San Jose, California to stay with Annie, one of Joe's daughters – flying over The Grand Canyon, much to Giuseppe's delight.

Annie took us to San Francisco for a tram ride and the following day, across the Golden Gate Bridge. Next stop was Alcatraz to see the cells of famous inmates-Al Capone and Robert Stroud, 'The Bird Man of Alcatraz.'

Flying back to Boston we felt the chill after the warmer climes of California and after spending another couple of days with the family, returned home: Elizabetta and Giuseppe to Italy, myself to Hampton.

At the end of the month I visited the Fazioli piano factory in Sacile, North East of Venice, for four days, one of a party of twenty, most of who were members of the Piano Tuners Association. Mr. Fazioli himself gave us a tour, mentioning that he thoroughly checks every piano personally before it leaves the factory.

My travelling companions loved Fazioli, both its architecture and its food.

They asked me what on earth had made me leave Italy. 'Love', I replied.

The object of that love celebrated her 70th Birthday on the 8th of June 2005.

At the end of July, Barbara went to be entertained at Brinsworth House once more, while Geno, his niece and I travelled to Italy again.

We stayed in Como with my friends Luigi and Silvana and their family, who organised a wonderful barbecue for us. Luigi told us that a few weeks earlier, he and his brother Alberto had gone to the Venetian region to buy 700 litres of Prosecco white wine: we seemed to be getting through most of it that night.

I noticed that when Karen wasn't looking, Luigi topped up her glass with the words "Drink as much as you like – we're not looking." Karen, meanwhile, was obviously enjoying Italian hospitality.

An evening stroll around the town took us past actor George Clooney's residence, Oleandra, situated at the side of the lake, while across the water another huge mansion was lit up, its lights reflected in the water: it was a luxurious international conference centre for VIPs.

After breakfast the following morning we drove to Bellagio to spend the morning exploring the steep and tiny streets, eating our lunch at the top of the hill overlooking the lake.

Then we drove on to Verona and a delightful central hotel situated close to the arena.

After a hearty supper in the square, delighting in the varied – and often bizarre – street entertainment, we joined the crowd in the arena to enjoy a new production of

La Boheme.	As always, the hundreds of tiny candles held by the audience flickered in the darkness. I was reminded of our family dash to Verona for Pavarotti years before.

Sightseeing the next day included Romeo and Juliet's balcony – in its graffiti covered courtyard – and shopping in the market and tiny souvenir shops.

After a night in Rimini we made for Bari: Karen had expressed a wish to see San Giovanni Rotondo where Padre Pio was buried. To get to this place of pilgrimage we had to drive to the top of the hill in temperatures of 42 degrees. As we reached a small village a few kilometres short of the top, the car suddenly stopped dead in protest. I decided to let it rest and cool off and opened the bonnet, as the screen readings gave me no idea what was wrong. After half an hour the car had regained its energy and we were able to proceed to the top, spending time in the church before continuing on to Cassano for a short stay.

From Cassano, we moved to a seaside residence we knew in Metaponto. It belonged to friends of ours who generously allowed us to use it. We spent a few days with Anthony, Khine and their children, who were staying in a hotel nearby and with my niece, Sandra and her family.

After a few days we said our goodbyes and made for the Amalfi coast with its stunning views, stopping in Vietri, Maiori and 'not to be missed' Ravello.

Don and I had visited the town on earlier travels, and I was keen that Geno and Karen should see its myriad of shops selling ceramics and its stunning views.

We finally reached Pompeii where we followed a private guided tour by a gentleman who approached us at the gate. He made the tour fascinating with his detailed knowledge and his anecdotes and ended it by showing us the 2000 year old arena. He demonstrated its acoustics by yelling into the space, his voice bouncing and echoing around the arena.

He also recommended a good hotel nearby and an excellent restaurant enjoyed, apparently, by the Pope and Andrea Boccelli amongst others – although presumably not all at the same time.

The next day we continued to Caserta and the Royal Palace which Don and I had so enjoyed previously. As we climbed into a horse-drawn carriage for a ride around the palace, the driver promised us a visit to the English Gardens. But the horse set off at a trot and we were back at the start before we knew it! Other carriages seemed to be proceeding at a gentler pace enabling their passengers to appreciate the view, while the animal pulling ours was obviously in a hurry. When we complained at the brevity of the 30 Euro ride and pointed out that we hadn't even seen the English Gardens, let alone enjoyed them, he told us that the gardens were closed and that he had to hurry because it was the horse's mealtime. Not knowing whether to be angry or amused we made sure that we added our story – and his – to the 'complaints' book.

Leaving Caserta behind, we drove towards the hill town of Spoleto, famous for its music festivals. It is twinned with Charleston USA by way of an annual event, 'The

Festival of the Two Worlds'.

The area is known for its savoury truffles, so the 'surprise menu' at dinner featured the very same in some form or another, and in every course – dessert included. The restaurant owner told us that his dog had been trained to sniff the truffles out in the local wood. Judging by the amount of truffles we consumed, he must have been something of an expert. That dog and his nose might have helped us find our way home that night: our evening stroll got us lost in the dark, and despite asking for directions and following a supposed 'shortcut' it took us some time to find our way back to the hotel.

After breakfast the following morning we visited the Basilica of St Francis at Assisi, and drove on to Siena, stopping en route at a town called Poggibonsi, simply because its name has always intrigued me!

We arrived in Siena just as there was going to be a rehearsal for the *Palio delle Contrade* – a horse race unique to the town – in the Piazza del Campo.

As we joined the crowds of people lining its margins to wait for the rehearsal to begin, a man behind us explained the origin of the *Palio* and its thousand year history. Each jockey, he explained, rides for his own *contrada* – or district – of Siena, wearing colours to represent that area. Each *contrada* also has its own individual 'race name', based on an animal or insect. There are no monetary prizes as each jockey races simply for a banner and the honour of the district he represents. The horses are chosen by drawing straws and blessed in a local church before the race begins; which is probably just as well: the race is very dangerous and very fast. The riding is reckless as jockeys risk injury to cut corners at great speed to get ahead of their rivals. The noise of cheering is deafening as the animals thunder past sending dust flying in pursuit of glory for their '*contrada*'.

Once the rehearsal was over, the horses and their jockeys paraded through the streets as a preview to the Big Day. We knew we wouldn't be able to stay in Siena to watch the real event, but felt privileged to have been there to at least witness the preparations.

The following day we drove towards Florence stopping at San Giminiano – famous for its tall towers – en route. Our hotel in Siena had booked us into a very central hotel close to the Duomo, so central that we had to drive through a 'pedestrians only' square to reach it. We were stopped by a *carbiniere* who asked us what on earth we thought we were doing. When we explained, he lifted his eyes heavenward in mock exclamation and kindly let us through.

After a dinner of Steak Florentine – what else? – we wandered through the narrow streets enjoying the entertainment, ending up on the Ponte Vecchio, the famous bridge whose multitude of jewellery shops line the bridge as it crosses the River Arno.

As we walked, we noticed a group of four of five teenagers who were sitting on the very edge of the bridge supports chatting and laughing. Their increasingly precarious position above the water suggested that they would end up in the river before

Chef Mario & helper from Australia, niece Isabella

the night was out.

The following day the queue for the Uffizi gallery was sadly too long for us to join, so we went to the Galleria del Academia to see Michelangelo's stunning sculpture of 'David'.

His imposing figure seemed to look beyond the assembled crowd with a quiet wisdom and nonchalance, his every muscle and vein exquisitely sculpted and larger than life.

Next, we waited in the queue for the Duomo, Brunellesci's masterpiece of a cathedral, enjoying the entertainment of the street vendors who spread out their wares at our feet, hoping to make a sale. They would keep one eye on potential customers and the other on the street, fearing the *carbinieri* who would be quick to move them on.

One evening, our after dinner stroll inevitably involved sampling some of the delicious ice creams sold by the city's abundance of excellent ice cream parlours. As many as twenty or thirty flavours of ice-cream are spread out in each shop making the choice almost arduous. From the pale green of pistachio through the speckled browns of cappuccino to the creamy rose of raspberry, a single scoop is never enough.

We left Florence the following day to return home, via a night's stay in Aosta, the closest town to Mount Blanc. We arrived home from our tour of Italy having clocked up three and a half thousand miles.

Barlow Road, Hampton. Sept 2006. From left: Daniel, Matteo, Nathan, Millie & Tullio.

2006 began happily with a visit from G1 and his brother-in-law, Nino. I collected them from Victoria station in the middle of the night and they opened their bags like smugglers to produce three two-litre bottles of red wine, two litres of olive oil and two kilos of parmesan cheese. G1 can always be relied upon to keep me well fed and watered the Italian way.

Mario & Barbara's grandchildren Massimo and Bali - Anthony's children

To celebrate their visit, I arranged a dinner party with friends, including Isa, and took them sightseeing in London. Another friend, Celia, offered to take them to tea at the Ritz but unfortunately G1 and Nino were dressed rather too casually to be allowed into such a refined environment. Thankfully, the waiter was Italian and soon had them kitted out appropriately, even if the jacket given to Nino, a tall man, looked as if it should belong to his child brother.

Isa, meanwhile, was in seventh heaven as she had always dreamed of having tea at the Ritz. She telephoned me afterwards brimming with excitement to say 'Guess where we've just been?!'

As Barbara's mental state continued to deteriorate, she was seen again by a number of doctors and a psychiatrist. They concluded that she did not seem mentally capable of answering the questions they asked and was increasingly confused. For Barbara's protection we decided to arrange a power of attorney. The implications of Barbara's situation were distressing and painfully sad, especially for those who loved her so much.

As we approached our 45th wedding anniversary and my 70th birthday, I had much to reflect upon.

25 May 2006. Mario & Rolf Harris at the Ivor Novello Music Awards

Barlow Road Hampton. Mario & Massimo

Afterword

Barbara and I have enjoyed many more years together than we had thought possible in those dark days of 1966. We have been able to 'live for the day' and travel widely. Her encouragement and support has enabled me to develop a career that has given me much pleasure and introduced me to so many people across the world, many of whom have become dear and treasured friends.

We have three wonderful sons of whom we are so proud. They have brought us both a great deal of joy and given us six bright and beautiful grandchildren. Every one, son and grandchild, shares our love of travel.

Music has carried me through my life: it gives me great pleasure, lifts my spirits, stimulates my mind and is a source of relaxation and meditation.

My memberships of the British Academy of Songwriters; The Musical Instrument Technology Institute and the Piano Tuners Association have always given me a sense of satisfaction and achievement.

In my teens I often wondered what I would do in the future. I knew that I wanted to move around so that I could meet different people, but I had no idea how. Yet the work I have done – still do now – has fulfilled those youthful dreams. I move from customer to customer and meet so many different people, many of whom have become my friends.

I was always in awe of my cousin Geno, who, unlike me had an academic background which began at Harvard University. I was astonished recently, when he expressed how much he admired me for my achievements: composing, travelling extensively and making the most of every opportunity.

The fact that I started my working life at a very young age, have lived in two countries, and seen as many others as possible, has been my 'university of life.'

Our marriage, although very happy, has sometimes seemed to be more about sickness than health and consequently often more to do with the worst than the best. Yet we have so many loving and happy memories. Perhaps suffering throws joy into greater, clearer relief.

As I write, it is fifty years since we met in that little bar in Rimini: Mario, the boy who never missed an opportunity to sing and Barbara, the beautiful English girl with the penetrating gaze, who would later join him on their wedding day with the words "Ciao Mario". Ours is a continuing story...